G000272458

Advanced
Vocabulary & Idiom

B J THOMAS

Pearson Education Limited
Edinburgh Gate, Harlow
Essex CM20 2JE, England
and Associated Companies throughout the world.

www.longman.com

© B J Thomas 1989

First published by Edward Arnold,
a division of Hodder and Stoughton Ltd 1989
ISBN 0-17-52952-0

Second and subsequent editions first published by Thomas Nelson and Sons Ltd 1990
ISBN 0-17-5556082-X

This (revised) edition published by Longman Group Limited 1995
Fifteenth impression 2009

ISBN 978-0-17-557126-0

All rights reserved. No part of this publication may be reproduced, stored in a retrieval system,
or transmitted in any form or by any means, electronic, mechanical, photocopying, recording or
otherwise, without the prior written permission of the Publishers.

Printed in Malaysia, PP
Illustrations by P Sheldon, Bill Lisle

Contents

Introduction

Advanced Vocabulary and Idiom is for students who already have a good command of the basic structures of English and who now wish to increase their range of vocabulary and idiom, and to gain more knowledge of particular styles of English. It gives invaluable assistance to students preparing for advanced examinations in English.

To the student

Advanced Vocabulary and Idiom presents words and phrases from a wide variety of topics and gives practice in different styles of English, such as formal, colloquial and slang, advertising and newspaper headlines. The types of exercises are varied and students are helped to understand not only what the words mean but also how they are used. Learners on their own should avoid going through the book mechanically. Exercises should be done at intervals and as a supplement to other materials and activities, and students should give themselves time to practise what they have learnt before going on to learn more. It is not satisfactory simply to complete the exercises and *understand* the new words in them. Learners must actually *use* the words in conversation, composition and letters before they can feel confident that these words are part of their active vocabulary.

To the teacher

Advanced Vocabulary and Idiom is divided into twelve sections, each concentrating on a different aspect of vocabulary and its use. Dictionary Practice is designed to increase students' awareness of the ways in which a dictionary can be used. Topics and Related Word Groups introduce new words and phrases as useful preparation for conversation and composition on given subjects. Word Formation contains exercises to increase awareness of how words are constructed. Problem Words is intended as a reference section to be used as and when problems arise with particular words and phrases. Idiom introduces groups of common idiomatic words and phrases, and requires students to put them in the contexts provided. Identification contains brief comprehension exercises in particularly areas of vocabulary. The Description exercises first provide practical comprehension practice based on certain kinds of common description, and then require students to use what they have learnt in this process by giving similar descriptions of their own. The exercises in Style assist students systematically to understand formal, colloquial and other more specialist forms of English and then, where it is useful, require them to produce the same kind of language themselves. Spoken English introduces certain common colloquial forms and will be especially useful for students who do not study in English-speaking countries and therefore do not have the advantage of hearing this kind of language around them. The Miscellaneous section contains a variety of exercises: Geo-political Names will help students to understand newspapers and other mass media; Names and Titles and Abbreviations give practical information about everyday English usage; Foreign Words and Phrases, Proverbs and Euphemisms provide useful knowledge of commonly-used expressions. Word Games provide entertaining puzzles.

Dictionary Practice

Use a good dictionary to do the following exercises. If you like, you can try to do them without help first, but check your answers in a dictionary afterwards.

Pronunciation

1   In each three-word group below, circle the two words which have the same-sounding underlined parts.

Examples: e.g. (finger) da**ng**er (hu**ng**er)   warn (farm) (part)

a)   **s**word **s**wear **s**witch
b)   qu**ay** pl**ay** **s**ee
c)   ou**gh**t **c**olonel thi**rd**
d)   b**o**ttle c**o**mpany fl**oo**d
e)   ti**mb**er nu**mb**er cli**mb**er

f)   ya**ch**t cau**gh**t h**o**t
g)   ri**se** advi**se** prac**tise**
h)   **th**eatre **th**ose **th**ink
i)   a**i**sle s**igh** d**a**te
j)   st**o**re c**oa**t l**ow**

2   In each of the four-word groups below, <u>two</u> words rhyme. Circle the rhyming pairs.

Examples: (beat) great (heat) sit   face (raise) (maze) pass

a)   phone done gone shone
b)   story lorry worry hurry
c)   bomb comb some dome
d)   saw owe go how
e)   hour four door throw

f)   show how rough though
g)   bough tough stuff grow
h)   hard word third lord
i)   lose loose choose chose
j)   piece prize nice rise

Stress

Mark the stressed syllable in each word below.

Examples: 'advertise   ad'vertisement   inde'pendent   'many

advise   guarantee   necessary   apostrophe
promise   central   necessitate   economic
educate   centralisation   necessarily   economist

Spelling

Finish the spelling of the words below with the correct endings from those above each group.

1   **-acy -asy -isy**
democr-   idiosyncr-   accur-   fant-   obstin-
ecst-   conspir-   priv-   diplom-   hypocr-

2   -able -eable -ible

port-	chang-	predict-	unpronounc-
respons-	sens-	knowledg-	uninhabit-
advis-	peac-	incorrupt-	convert-

3   -ious -eous

court-	erron-	ted-	grac-	miscellan-
glor-	gorg-	hid-	infect-	relig-

Meaning

1   Finish each phrase on the left with the most suitable item on the right.

1) She carved	a) the ordeal.
2) He felled	b) the garden.
3) She weeded	c) a school.
4) He founded	d) the tree.
5) She survived	e) the joint.

2   Arrange the words below into groups of equal number, each group containing related words.

bowler	brakes	bridge	crawl	limp
busby	boot	beret	account	bumpers
hull	balance	cap	stroll	dashboard
helmet	statement	porthole	deposit	windscreen
deck	overdraft	funnel	stagger	creep

3   In each five-word group below, four words are similar in meaning and one is completely different. Circle the 'odd one out' in each group, and say why it does not belong.

Example: foe   rival   (ally)   adversary   opponent

Answer: The others all mean 'enemy, someone against you'.

a) pal	mate	buddy	dimwit	chum
b) swift	fleet	sluggish	nifty	brisk
c) adore	abhor	detest	loathe	despise
d) peak	zenith	nadir	apex	summit
e) soaked	saturated	drenched	sopping	parched
f) plead	appeal	implore	entreat	grant

Word Parts

1   Give the irregular plurals of these words.

goose   salmon   mouse   oasis
ox   aircraft   half   diagnosis

2   Put the correct form of the word in brackets in each sentence below.

a) He's been very _____ and bad-tempered recently. (quarrel)
b) The six _____ finally reached the summit. (mountain)
c) The park is roughly _____ in shape. (triangle)
d) Thanks for the book. It was very _____. (inform)

3   Make compound nouns or adjectives, using the word on the left as the first part, to fit the meanings given.

Example: finger (mark left by a finger) = fingerprint

fire   (organisation which puts out fires)
    (that cannot burn, catch fire)
    (gun, rifle, pistol, etc.)

light   (tower with light to warn ships at sea)
    (happy, without worries)
    (liable to steal)

play   (portable enclosure for a baby)
    (rich man devoted to pleasure)
    (person who writes plays)

Word Use

1   Put the correct prepositions in these sentences.

a) He abstained _____ voting.   c) She's engrossed _____ the book.
b) I divided it _____ six parts.   d) I'm disgusted _____ his behaviour.

2   The verbs in the sentences below are used without an object, i.e. intransitively. Some of them can also be used with an object, i.e. transitively. Where possible, add the object in brackets.

Examples We ate in silence. (the meal)   He fell to the ground. (the book).
    We ate the meal in silence.   No object possible. (We cannot say: He fell the book to the ground.)

a) I leant against the wall. (my bike)
b) She walked in the park. (the dog)
c) He drives very carefully. (his taxi)
d) She knelt in the church. (her children)
e) She sat on the chair. (the baby)
f) He lay on the floor. (the books)
g) He marched up the hill. (his men)
h) They arrived at seven. (the car)

Topics

City Life

Put each of the following words or phrases in its correct place in the passage.

cosmopolitan	pollution	congestion	to breed crime
metropolis	urban	cost of living	irresistible lure
stimulation	commuter	city-dwellers	anonymity

Most people in developed countries are (a) _____, many drawn by the (b) _____ of the (c) _____. The attractions of the city are many: the (d) _____ atmosphere (foreign restaurants, different languages, international companies), the (e) _____ of cultural events or the simple hope of finding work. All too many find, however, that the glamorous façade is false. One can be very alone in the city and the (f) _____ which at first seems to give freedom and protection later leaves just loneliness. There is a lot to do but everything is expensive. The (g) _____ is high. There is (h) _____ not only of the physical but also of the moral environment and the various pressures of (i) _____ life cause cities (j) _____. Above all, perhaps, it is the daily stresses and strains of the city which make life there a matter of survival rather than of enjoyment. Many a (k) _____ struggling to work through the rush-hour (l) _____ asks, 'Is it worth it?'

Issues of Education

Put each of the following words or phrases in its correct place in the passage.

elite	divisive	potential	gifted
classless	spontaneity	cram	streaming
conventional	labelled	privileged	inferiority complex

It is interesting that in some countries which are socialist and therefore supposedly (a) _____, the educational system is based on (b) _____, which means that children are educated according to their ability, with the more (c) _____ children separated from the others. Supporters of this system say that more intelligent children will be helped to achieve their full (d) _____ in this way and that these children will be held back if they have to share lessons with less clever pupils. Opponents of this system, on the other hand, maintain that it creates an educated (e) _____, a special class of (f) _____ people who are encouraged to think of themselves as superior to the others. Similarly the others may, as a result of being (g) _____ second-rate, develop some kind of (h) _____. In a word, such a system is (i) _____, since it creates a division between people. Another important question in education is the amount of freedom and choice children should be given at school. The conservative view is that a (j) _____ system of strict rules is best. However, critics of this attitude say it causes regimentation, as in the army, and discourages children's natural imagination and (k) _____. We must ask ourselves what the purpose of education is: to (l) _____ children's heads with facts or to encourage them to develop their natural abilities in their own way?

Fashion in Clothes

Put each of the following words or phrases in its correct place in the passage.

slavishly	trends	slaves to fashion
individualists	trendy	fashion houses
conformists	dictate	the latest fashion
haute couture	dictates	personal ornaments

Most people like to think they are (a) _____ and simply wear whatever they like. Few people will admit to being (b) _____. However we are not just talking of the expensive (c) _____ of the Paris and Milan (d) _____, which not many people can afford anyway. We are talking of fashions and (e) _____ in everyday clothes. We say that we wear jeans and sweaters because they are cheap and practical, but isn't it true that our jeans and sweaters tend to be the same as everyone else wears? Doesn't that mean that we like to be (f) _____? Of course the big chain-stores, to some extent, (g) _____ what we wear, but they always offer a choice and people do, on the whole, like to wear (h) _____, which extends beyond clothes to make-up, (i) _____ (men wear earrings too, nowadays) and hair styles. It is easy to declare that we do not (j) _____ follow the (k) _____ of fashion, but aren't we all (l) _____ at heart?

The Environment

Put each of the following words or phrases in its correct place below.

sewage	enlightened	pesticides	sustainable
organic	acid rain	ecological	deforestation
disposal	herbicides	extinction	animal rights

When industrialisation began, little thought was given to its (a) _____ effects. Raw, untreated (b) _____ was allowed to pollute our seas and rivers. Animals were killed for profit to the point of (c) _____. The loss of trees through uncontrolled (d) _____ caused erosion and unstable climate. (e) _____ was caused by the poisonous gases man sent into the atmosphere. Chemicals in (f) _____ killed animal life. (g) _____ destroyed plants. The balance of nature was disturbed.

It is only now that we are waking up to the problem. More natural, (h) _____ farming is advocated. Legislation controls the (i) _____ of waste products into our air and water. Wildlife organisations are becoming more militant in their fight for (j) _____. Replanting policies in some parts of the world mean that our forests should in future be (k) _____.

We can only hope that growing public awareness and (l) _____ legislation will produce a world which is safe for us and will provide a good quality of life for future generations.

Advertising

Put each of the following words or phrases in its correct place below.

beneficial	misleading	blatant	brainwash
implicit	catchy jingles	exploit	ubiquitous
bombard	watchdog	subtle	informative

Modern advertisements contain hidden messages. (a) _____ in the advertisement showing the pretty girl in the new car or the smiling children round the packet of washing powder is the message that if we buy the product, we also achieve success and happiness. It is a (b) _____ approach since it seeks to (c) _____ our secret dreams, and it is inescapable since advertising is (d) _____. Giant street hoardings and (e) _____ on television (f) _____ us from all sides. They (g) _____ us into believing that we can realise our ambitions quickly and easily. On the other hand, defenders of advertising say that it is (h) _____. Advertising is (i) _____. Advertisements tell us about useful new products. They brighten our lives with colour and music. They increase demand, stimulate industry and so keep prices down. Whether for or against advertising, most people would agree that some kind of (j) _____ body, appointed by the government or by the advertising industry itself, is necessary to maintain standards of honesty and to discourage the more (k) _____ types of (l) _____ advertisements.

How Much Freedom Should Children Have?

Put each of the following words or phrases in its correct place below.

possessive	upbringing	permissive	rebelliousness
suppress	formative	adolescence	run wild
inhibited	authoritarian	juvenile delinquency	

It is often said that we live in a (a) _____ age, one in which people are allowed to do almost anything they like. Is this good for children? They are going through their (b) _____, which is a very (c) _____ stage of their development since their final adult characters are beginning to take shape. Some parents think it is good for children to be allowed to (d) _____, without control or supervision. They say that this enables children's personalities to develop naturally and that they will learn to be responsible by the mistakes they make. However, this might lead to (e) _____, with the children ending up in the courts, or it might simply make children self-centred, without any consideration for others. Other parents believe in being strict, but taken to extremes this can produce a too (f) _____ atmosphere in the home, with the children being dominated and ruled by their parents. Parents can also be very (g) _____ and try to keep their children dependent on them. These last two attitudes can encourage (h) _____ (against parents, school, authority) in a child, or, conversely, (i) _____ a child's natural sense of adventure and curiosity. A strict (j) _____ by over-caring parents can make a child so timid and (k) _____ that he or she is unable to express freely his or her emotions and form mature relationships. To bring up children to be normal, well-adjusted human beings requires great wisdom, and perhaps a bit of luck.

Censorship

Put each of the following words or phrases in its correct place below.

moral standards **perverted** **banned** **masquerading**
unscrupulous **excessive** **degrádes** **safeguards**
counter-productive **infringes** **corrupting** **gratuitous**

The amount of offensive material we are exposed to in films nowadays is surely (a) _____. Most people accept that scenes of sex and violence are sometimes necessary to tell a story, but all too often these scenes are (b) _____; they are unnecessary and simply inserted in the film to appeal to the baser human instincts. Censorship is necessary, especially to protect children from the (c) _____ influence of such scenes, often (d) _____ as art, in our cinemas. There should also be censorship of pornographic magazines produced by (e) _____ people willing to cater to the (f) _____ tastes of a small minority. Such material destroys the innocence of the young and (g) _____ all who read it. On the other hand, there are those who say that something which is (h) _____ becomes desirable so censorship is (i) _____, and that censorship (j) _____ on our freedom of choice. However freedom is not merely freedom to do what we want but freedom from attempts to destroy society's (k) _____. Censorship provides the (l) _____ by which society protects itself.

Love

Put each of the following words in its correct place below.

partners **platonic** **flirtation** **infatuation**
mature **compatible** **one-sided** **hero-worship**
mutual **idolize** **complement** **stable**

Youngsters in their teens or even earlier sometimes (a) _____ film stars or other celebrities with a kind of blind, devoted (b) _____. The objects of such adoration are regarded as gods by their smitten worshippers. How sad that such devotion is almost always unrequited (though pop-stars have been known to marry their fans). Young people also sometimes develop an irrational obsession for another, often older, person which is not an adult, (c) _____ feeling but simply a youthful (d) _____. At parties a boy may playfully try to attract a girl, or vice versa, without intending any serious, lasting relationship. This is just a (e) _____. A relationship which gives deep and lasting happiness to both (f) _____ must not be (g) _____ (felt more strongly by one of the pair than by the other). It should be based on a (h) _____ love and respect, felt equally by each of the two. Of course it can take many forms. It might be very deep but entail no physical desire, in which case it is described as (i) _____. Certainly, for any relationship to be (j) _____, the two people involved must be (k) _____ (they must get on well together). This does not necessarily mean that they must have attitudes and interests in common, for partnerships of opposites can work very well. The different characters of the two people somehow (l) _____ each other.

Attitudes to Work and Leisure

Put each of the following words or phrases in its correct place below.

constructively	rewarding	challenge	conditioned
aimless	initiative	creativity	9 to 5
regimentation	scope	aspire	fulfilment

Most adults (a) _____ to more leisure but, in fact, not many people have the necessary (b) _____ to use the free time they already have very (c) _____. The sad fact is that we need work because it imposes the discipline we need. Life seems (d) _____ and we secretly look forward to our work again. We dream about personal (e) _____ but probably find it more in our work than in our leisure time. This depends on age. The young are free from work and responsibility, and freedom comes naturally to them. However, after they begin jobs they become (f) _____ to work. They find they need it, however much they complain about its routine and (g) _____. Obviously this again depends on the kind of work. Those with (h) _____ jobs, or jobs which require (i) _____, receive genuine satisfaction from their work, but most of us are in conventional (j) _____ jobs which offer little (k) _____ for imagination. We leave our work only to face a leisure that we find difficult to cope with. Our mistake is in regarding leisure as a chance to do nothing, whereas in fact it should be looked on as a (l) _____.

The Purpose of State Punishment

Put each of the following words or phrases in its correct place below.

wrongdoer	deterrent	law-abiding	death penalty
misdeeds	reform	humane	rehabilitate
barbaric	retribution	crime doesn't pay	corporal punishment

What is the purpose of punishment? One purpose is obviously to (a) _____ the offender, to correct the offender's moral attitudes and anti-social behaviour and to (b) _____ him or her, which means to assist the offender to return to normal life as a useful member of the community. Punishment can also be seen as a (c) _____, because it warns other people of what will happen if they are tempted to break the law and so prevents them from doing so. However, a third purpose of punishment lies, perhaps, in society's desire for (d) _____, which basically means revenge. In other words, don't we feel that a (e) _____ should suffer for his (f) _____? The form of punishment should also be considered. On the one hand, some believe that we should 'make the punishment fit the crime'. Those who steal from others should be deprived of their own property to ensure that criminals are left in no doubt that (g) '_____'. For those who attack others, (h) _____ should be used. Murderers should be subject to the principle 'an eye for an eye and a tooth for a tooth' and automatically receive the (i) _____. On the other hand, it is said that such views are unreasonable, cruel and (j) _____ and that we should show a more (k) _____ attitude to punishment and try to understand why a person commits a crime and how society has failed to enable him to live a respectable, (l) _____ life.

Related Word Groups

Body

Divide the following 24 words into three equal groups under the headings
a) head b) arm and hand c) leg and foot.

jaw	lash	pupil	lobe	elbow
shin	temple	knuckles	calf	forearm
wrist	toes	thigh	thumb	heel
gums	biceps	instep	fist	ankle
lid	palm	sole	nostril	

Books

Types of Book

1   Put each of the following words in its correct place below.

volume	publication	whodunnit	hardback
best-seller	thriller	copy	edition
manuscript	proofs	paperback	

(a)   You can see the original _____ of *Hamlet* in the museum in Shakespeare's own writing.
(b)   Before a book is sent to be printed, the author must check the _____.
(c)   Where is _____ three of this set of encyclopaedias?
(d)   The new government report on agricultural statistics is a very interesting _____.
(e)   Have you got a _____ of Graham Greene's *Brighton Rock*?
(f)   This book costs £12, but that's the _____ price. The _____ costs only £5.50.
(g)   His first three novels didn't sell very well, but his fourth was a _____ and made a fortune.
(h)   The book has already been selling well for five years. Now the publishers are going to bring out a new _____ with illustrations.
(i)   She likes to relax by reading a _____ about spies or crime.
(j)   I'm reading a _____. It's fun trying to guess who the murderer is.

2   Answer the following questions using the words at the top of the exercise above. E.g. What might a publisher do if one of his books is chosen as a school or exam test? He might bring out a special *edition* with notes and test questions.
(a)   Why is an encyclopaedia usually more expensive than a dictionary?
(b)   What is a murder mystery called, and why?
(c)   What is an exciting adventure story called, and why?
(d)   How can you get information about scientific, technical, statistical and similar matters?
(e)   How would you ask for a particular book in a bookshop?
(f)   What must an author do when a publisher's deadline arrives?
(g)   What must be done before a book is printed?
(h)   What does every author hope?
(i)   How can you save money when buying books?

Ways of reading

3   Put each of the following words or phrases into its correct place in the sentences below.

skip	look up	browse	refer to	flip through
skim	dip into	peruse	wade through	read from cover to cover

(a)   I spend a lot of time in bookshops. I don't often buy books. I just _____.
(b)   If I come to a boring bit in a book, I just _____ a few pages till the real story starts again.
(c)   I'll _____ his number in the phone-book.
(d)   I didn't know the word. I had to _____ a dictionary.
(e)   Of course an encyclopaedia is not a book you _____. You just _____ it for things that interest you.
(f)   I never liked history at school. I found it very hard to _____ all that boring stuff about wars and revolutions.
(g)   We have requested our lawyers to _____ the document with the greatest care to decide whether it's legal or not.
(h)   Some people have the ability to _____ a page, which means to read it very quickly, just taking in the main points.
(i)   I sometimes _____ a magazine in a newsagent's but I don't usually buy one.

4   Using one or more items from the list at the top of the exercise above, explain how you use each of the following. E.g. a novel. If it's good, I *read* it *from cover to cover*, but sometimes I *skip* long, descriptive passages.

a dictionary	a guidebook	an encyclopaedia
a magazine	an atlas	a photograph album
a newspaper	a contract	a car maintenance manual

5   Answer the questions below from the following list of parts of a book.

acknowledgements	'blurb'	key	glossary
contents	footnotes	chronology	appendix
dedication	frontispiece	index	bibliography

In what part of a book would you look to find ...
(a)   ... answers to exercise questions?
(b)   ... who supplied the photographs or helped with special research?
(c)   ... quickly what the book is about?
(d)   ... meanings of foreign or technical expressions used in the text?
(e)   ... on what page a person, place or event is mentioned?
(f)   ... if the book was written for a particular person?
(g)   ... extra information about something mentioned in the main text?
(h)   ... what other books have been written on the same subject?
(i)   ... a picture of the author or the subject of the book?
(j)   ... how the book is organised in chapters?
(k)   ... a convenient list of the dates and events of the period covered in the book?

Dirt and Damage

1   Put each of the following adjectives in its correct place in the sentences.

blunt	**scratched**	**smeared**	**shabby**
torn	**shop-soiled**	**filthy**	**soiled**
rusty	**stained**	**smudged**	**faded**

(a)   He was very angry when he saw that his new car was _____. Another car must have run along the side of it.

(b)   The curtains were bright red when we bought them, but they've become _____ in the strong sunlight.

(c)   That jacket needs cleaning and it's rather old. I think it's too _____ to wear.

(d)   If you have a banknote which is _____ in two, take it to a bank and exchange it for a new one.

(e)   Buy our new design 'Travelbag'. The different compartments will enable the traveller to keep clean and _____ garments separate.

(f)   When she was two years old, she used to experiment with her mother's lipstick. Her face was always _____ with it.

(g)   See those red-brown bits? That's where the machine is beginning to go _____ because it's unprotected from the rain.

(h)   You can see the ceiling is _____ where the rain came through.

(i)   This radio is a bit _____ after being in the shop for nine months, so I'll knock 10% off the price.

(j)   Let the ink dry before you put another piece of paper on top of it. Otherwise it'll be _____.

(k)   This knife isn't sharp, it's _____. Give me another one.

(l)   This shirt isn't just dirty, Bobby. It's absolutely _____!

2   Using the words from the list at the top of the exercise above, say what kind of damage or wear the following items can suffer.

a photograph	a book	a car in an accident
a coat	a razor-blade	a car after long use
a television set	a piece of furniture	

'POSH'

'Posh' means 'smart', 'upper-class'. It is said that the word originated when wealthy people travelled by ship to and from India when it was under British rule. To avoid the hot sun in the Indian Ocean during the voyage, the richer passengers specified that their cabins should be on the left side ('port') of the ship going out to India, and on the right side ('starboard') on the way home. Port Out, Starboard Home: POSH.

Drinking

1   Make sentences by connecting each person on the left below with the correct phrase on the right.

(a)   A teetotaller   serves people in a pub.
(b)   A secret drinker   runs a pub.
(c)   A social drinker   has a drink from time to time.
(d)   An occasional drinker   only drinks with other people, e.g. at parties.
(e)   An alcoholic   doesn't want other people to know he drinks.
(f)   A drunkard   drinks a lot.
(g)   A 'wino'   is often drunk.
(h)   A heavy drinker   never drinks alcohol.
(i)   A publican   produces beer in large quantities.
(j)   A barman   is addicted to alcohol.
(k)   A brewer   is a poor person, often homeless, who drinks anything, anywhere.

2   The dangers of alcoholism are very real. Put the people in the above exercise (on the left) in order of the danger they are in from alcoholism, with those in greatest danger at the top. Then draw a line between those you think are safe from alcoholism and those who might become, or already are, in danger from this disease.

3   Match each drink on the left below with its description on the right.

(a)   squash   a last (alcoholic) drink before going to bed
(b)   a cocktail   a non-alcoholic fruit drink
(c)   a nightcap   a mixture of beer and lemonade (or a similar drink)
(d)   one for the road   a mixture of wine or spirits and hot water, sugar, lemon etc.
(e)   a shandy   a refreshing non-alcoholic drink, e.g. squash, Coca-Cola
(f)   punch   a single drink of spirits
(g)   a soft drink   a mixed alcoholic drink
(h)   a short   a last drink before driving

4   From the list of drinks on the left above, choose one or more which would be a good drink for ...
        ... a children's party.
        ... an adults' party.
        ... a formal reception.
        ... someone who's going to drive.
        ... a last drink of the evening.
        ... a hot day.
        ... someone who is nervous before an important occasion.
        ... someone who is trying to give up alcohol.

5   Put each of the following words into its correct place in the sentences.

sip	pub crawl	toast	breathalyzer
drop	stagger	booze	corkscrew
intoxicated	vineyard	cheers	hangover

(a)   Let's open another bottle of wine. Where's the _____?
(b)   We went on a _____ last night. This morning I've got a terrible _____.
(c)   Wine is made from grapes, which are grown in a _____.

(d) Here's a _____ to John and Elizabeth.
(e) Don't drink it all at once. Just _____ it.
(f) When British people drink, they often say, '_____'.
(g) The police stopped the driver and gave him a _____ test.
(h) I don't want much, please, just a _____.
(i) A slang word for alcoholic drink is '_____'.
(j) A formal word for 'drunk' is '_____'.
(k) He couldn't walk properly. He could only _____.

6   Briefly describe, as a warning of the possible dangers of alcohol, an evening in which some people start drinking and end up in a police cell. Use at least six of the words at the top of the exercise above.

7   Explain the difference in each of the following pairs.
(a) sober and drunk
(b) tipsy and drunk
(c) still orange and fizzy orange
(d) draught beer and bottled beer
(e) 'on the wagon' and teetotal
(f) vintage wine and 'plonk'
(g) a pub and an off-licence
(h) neat whisky and whisky 'on the rocks'
(i) 'Dutch courage' and 'to go Dutch'

Driving

1   Put each of the following verbs, in the past tense, in its correct place in the passage below.

accelerate	fasten	pull up	sound
adjust	dip	release	skid
apply	indicate	reverse	start up
check	overtake	swerve	turn on

Another hundred miles to go. Dark night. Heavy traffic. He glanced at the dashboard. He was OK for fuel and well within the speed-limit. He (a) _____ that he was pulling out, put his foot down, (b) _____ and (c) _____ two cars in front. It began to rain. He (d) _____ the windscreen wipers and settled back comfortably into the leather upholstery. For a moment he was mesmerised by the rhythmic movement of the wipers. He looked at the road ahead. An oncoming car! He (e) _____ his head-lights but was dazzled by the other driver's. He (f) _____ his horn. The other car seemed to be coming straight towards him! He (g) _____ to avoid it. He was confused. He (h) _____ his brakes, but (i) _____ on the wet surface. He went off the road and collided with a tree. Slowly he (j) _____ onto the road again, drove ten metres forward and (k) _____. He got out and inspected the car for damage. Some scratches on the bodywork. Dented bumper. He lifted the bonnet and (l) _____ the engine. It appeared to be OK. He got into the car again, (m) _____ his seat-belt, (n) _____ the mirror and (o) _____ the engine nervously. It purred sweetly. Good. He (p) _____ the hand-brake. The car moved forward. Another hundred miles to go.

2   Describe how you failed your driving test disastrously.

Food

Ways of Eating

1   Put each of the following verbs into its correct place in the sentences.

chew	lick	polish off	swallow	gnaw
consume	peck at	gorge	digest	bolt

(a)   The children have no appetite. They just _____ their food. They hardly eat anything.

(b)   My mother always used to say to me. 'Now make sure you _____ meat carefully before you _____ it.'

(c)   Statistics show that we _____ more fruit and meat than 10 years ago.

(d)   He has an enormous appetite. I've seen him _____ four hamburgers and a pile of chips at a sitting.

(e)   As children we used to _____ ourselves on ice-cream, chips and chocolate, and then feel very sick.

(f)   The starving prisoners were so desperate they would _____ any meat bones they could find.

(g)   It's not good for your body to _____ your food so quickly. Eat slowly so that you can _____ it properly.

(h)   He was so hungry that when he'd finished his food, he began to _____ the plate!

2   Answer the following questions using words from the list at the top of Exercise 1.

How do people eat ice-cream cones?
How do hungry people eat?
How do very greedy people eat?
How do people eat if they are not very hungry?
How do dogs eat?
What is a good, healthy way to eat meat?
What is an unhealthy way to eat, and why?

Meats

3   Some meat is given a different name from the animal it comes from. What animals do the following meats come from?

(a)   pork
(b)   beef
(c)   bacon
(d)   venison

(e)   veal
(f)   mutton
(g)   ham

Food preparation

4   Match each verb on the left below with the food item on the right it is most often associated with.

(a) to pluck   cheese
(b) to crack   an orange
(c) to grate   a chicken
(d) to knead   a nut
(e) to peel   a rabbit
(f) to skin   a joint of meat
(g) to slice   dough
(h) to carve   a loaf

5   Instructions as above.

(a) to mince   cream
(b) to shell   meat
(c) to toss   a hard-boiled egg
(d) to whip   eggs
(e) to stuff   a cake
(f) to mash   a chicken
(g) to beat   a pancake
(h) to ice   potatoes

6   Explain the difference between the words or phrases in each of the following pairs.

(a) starving and parched
(b) a snack and a square meal
(c) stale and mouldy
(d) peckish and ravenous
(e) uneatable and inedible
(f) a beer-bottle and a bottle of beer
(g) a starter and a dessert
(h) a restaurant and a café

COCKNEY RHYMING SLANG

The Cockneys of the East End of London devised their own slang, making words and phrases, still used, which rhymed with the normal words.

apples and pears (stairs)
trouble and strife (wife)
plates of meat (feet)
rub-a-dub (pub)
loaf of bread (head)
dicky-bird (word)

whistle and flute (suit)
frog and toad (road)
north and south (mouth)
butcher's hook (look)
Rosy Lee (tea)
Joanna (piano)

The problem, however, in trying to guess the meanings of these words is that the rhyming part is often dropped and people simply say:
'What's that? Let's have a **butcher's.**'
'Come on! Use your **loaf!**'
'That's a nice **whistle** you're wearing.'

Friends

1   The following is a list of different kinds of friends (and a few associates and enemies). Put each one in the most suitable space in the sentences below. Some words must be used more than once.

acquaintance	foe	associate	old flame
compatriot	partner	bosom pal	fair-weather friend
confidant	mate	pen-pal	colleague
companion	rival		

(a)   She comes from the same country as me. She's a _____.
(b)   We carried on a friendship through letters. He was a _____.
(c)   I'd rather not make the journey alone. I need a travelling-_____.
(d)   He and I own this business together. He's my _____.
(e)   She didn't know what the homework was so she asked a class-_____.
(f)   I've known George for ages. We're really good old friends who spend a lot of time together. He's my _____.
(g)   Henry Somers wants the manager's job and so do I. He's my _____.
(h)   Wanted: sensible, well-mannered girl to act as old lady's _____.
(i)   She used to be John's girl-friend. She's an _____.
(j)   The assistant to a plumber, electrician or lorry driver is known as his _____.
(k)   In the darkness the soldier couldn't see whether the approaching figure was friend or _____.
(l)   She teaches in the same school as I do. She's a _____.
(m)   He seems a good friend when things are going well, but when I'm in trouble he's nowhere to be seen. I'm afraid he's a _____.
(n)   He's the person to whom I tell my most personal thoughts, problems and fears. He's my _____.
(o)   If you can't afford to live on your own, you'll have to find a flat-_____.
(p)   I don't really know him very well. He's just an _____.
(q)   I just meet him occasionally when his firm and my firm work together. He's just a business _____.

2   Which people from the list at the top of the exercise above would you ...
   ... talk business with?   ... not trust?
   ... go to with personal problems?   ... borrow money from?
   ... visit on holiday?   ... invite to your party?
   ... go on holiday with?   ... invite to your wedding?

ADJECTIVES FROM FAMOUS PEOPLE

The writer George Orwell, in *Animal Farm* and *1984,* warned of the dangers of totalitarian government, and we still describe that form of dictatorship as 'Orwellian'. Other examples of names becoming adjectives are Shakespearean, Victorian, Christian, Shavian (from Shaw) and Dickensian. Do you know the adjectives from these names? (They don't all end in '-an'.)

Churchill, Machiavelli, Napoleon, Mao, Elizabeth, Stalin, Hitler, Confucius, Lenin, Kafka, Thatcher, Freud, Ritz, Marx, Plato

Light

1 Put each word in its correct space in the sentences below.

flicker   **twinkle**   **flash**   **glow**   **lightning**
spark   **dazzle**   **sparkle** **flare**   **floodlight**

(a) The town council has decided to _____ the castle in summer for the benefit of tourists.
(b) Stand back when I put petrol on the fire. It will make it _____ up.
(c) I saw the _____ of a lighted cigarette in the darkness.
(d) He was killed by a _____ of _____ during a thunderstorm.
(e) The stars do not give off a constant light. They seem to _____.
(f) Put on dark glasses or the sun will _____ you and you won't be able to see.
(g) The candle flame began to _____ a little in the wind.
(h) In very dry weather just a small _____ from a passing train can start a forest fire.
(i) Look how the jewels in her crown _____ as she moves.

2 Instructions as above.

spotlight   **chandelier**   **traffic-lights**   **searchlight**
limelight   **torch**   **son et lumière**   **headlights**
footlights   **lantern**

(a) It was too dark to drive safely without the _____ on.
(b) The bus stopped at the _____.
(c) The usherette showed us to our seats in the cinema with her _____.
(d) Every summer they have a _____ show at Edinburgh Castle for tourists.
(e) Famous people spend their lives in the _____.
(f) The _____ in a theatre are along the front of the stage.
(g) She was illuminated in the middle of the dark stage by a single _____.
(h) The anti-aircraft unit used a powerful _____ to light up the sky and show any enemy planes.
(i) The large room was very grand. It was lit by an enormous _____ containing about 200 lights.
(j) 200 years ago, if you went out at night you carried a _____, which was a candle or oil-light inside a metal and glass container.

PALINDROMES

The words **mum, toot, deed, sexes** and **redder** all read the same backwards. They are called 'palindromes', which can also be sentences or longer pieces. The first man may have introduced himself to Eve with the words, **'Madam, I'm Adam'**. Arriving in exile, Napoleon could have said, **'Able was I ere I saw Elba'**. To celebrate a great new waterway: **A man, a plan, a canal – Panama**. Others are: **Was it a cat I saw?** And finally a long one:
Doc, note, I dissent. A fast never prevents a fatness. I diet on cod.

Materials

1 Match each material on the left below with the most appropriate word, phrase or phrases on the right.

(a)	corduroy	a ship's sail, a boxing ring
(b)	canvas	church windows
(c)	denim	the roof of a shed or cheap hut
(d)	fur	comfortable soft trousers
(e)	frosted glass	jeans
(f)	stained glass	bathroom windows
(g)	corrugated iron	a woman's expensive, warm coat
(h)	straw	cutlery
(i)	brick	a man's old-fashioned light summer hat
(j)	stainless steel	a wall

2 Instructions as above.

(a)	cork	old ships
(b)	silk	packing material
(c)	suede	fine cups, saucers, dishes
(d)	linen	a wine-bottle stopper
(e)	serge	shoes, a casual jacket
(f)	corrugated cardboard	a lawn
(g)	tweed	a woman's expensive evening dress
(h)	porcelain	fine bed-sheets
(i)	timber	a man's hard-wearing sports-jacket
(j)	turf	an ordinary soldier's uniform

3 What materials, from those in the exercises above, might the following items be made of?

a football pitch
a man's tie
table-mats
the lining of a winter coat
a woman's casual skirt
tents
a household lamp base
a dentist's surgery windows

a watch-case
a table-cloth
an overcoat
a house
an oil-painting base
a woman's purse
a cheap casual jacket
a baby's toy animal

AMERICAN ENGLISH 1

Once you are accustomed to the American accent, there should be no difficulty in understanding, and being understood by, speakers of American English. Here are some common words from American vocabulary. What words would British people use in their place?

store	apartment	sidewalk	trunk (car)
faucet	down-town	freshman	hood (car)
mailman	thumb tack	garbage	movie-theater
candy	gas (car)	elevator	stand in line

Money

Coins, notes and banks

1   Put each of the following words or phrases in its correct place in the sentences below.

numismatist   **standing order**   **currency**   **expenditure**
counterfoil   **counterfeit**   **statement**   **bounce**
legal tender

(a)   You can change your _____ at any bank or large hotel.
(b)   She held the note up to the light to make sure it wasn't _____.
(c)   He collects coins and banknotes. He's a _____.
(d)   I always fill in the _____ when I write out a cheque. Otherwise I would lose track of my _____.
(e)   I don't trust him. I'm sure his cheque will _____.
(f)   I pay my rent by _____. It saves me having to write a cheque every month.
(g)   The bank sends me a detailed _____ every month.
(h)   Don't worry. Scottish banknotes are _____ in England too.

Personal spending

2   Instructions as above.

broke   **quid**   **hire purchase**   **make ends meet**
mortgage   **I.O.U.**   **chickenfeed**   **instalments**

(a)   I'm afraid I have no money at all. I'm completely _____.
(b)   She finds London very expensive. She says she can't _____ on less than £100 a week.
(c)   To a multi-millionaire £100 is _____.
(d)   Can you lend me a couple of _____?
(e)   I managed to get a _____ to buy a house. I'll be paying it back for the next 20 years.
(f)   He lent me the money but he didn't trust me completely and asked me to give him an _____.
(g)   I couldn't really afford the car so I got it on _____ and paid monthly _____ until it was finally mine.

3   Use at least five of the words at the top of the above exercise and any you like from Exercise 1 to describe, in a short paragraph, someone's terrible financial situation.

TYPING PRACTICE

What is special about the following sentences?

The quick brown fox jumps over the lazy dog.
Pack my box with five dozen liquor jugs.
Jackdaws love my big sphinx of quartz.

Numbers

Put each of the following words in its correct place in the sentences below.

digits	**round**	**even**	**ordinal**	**scores**
Roman	**good**	**cardinal**	**odd**	**dozen**
average	**gross**	**odd**		

(a) It was after midnight but there were still _____ of people in the streets.
(b) 1, 2, 3, 4, 5 etc. are _____ numbers. 1st, 2nd, 3rd, 4th, 5th etc. are _____ numbers.
(c) Could you go and buy a _____ eggs, please?
(d) Each packet contains a _____ of paper-clips.
(e) I, II, III IV etc. are known as _____ numerals.
(f) 2, 4, 6, 8, 10 etc. are _____ numbers. 1, 3, 5, 7, 9 etc. are _____ numbers.
(g) There are normally seven _____ in a London telephone number.
(h) There were twenty-_____ people at the meeting. I don't know exactly how many.
(i) It was a bargain. I paid £10 but it was worth a _____ fifteen.
(j) The students' ages vary. The _____ is about 22.
(k) OK, I'll lend you the £95 you need. Well, let's make it a _____ number. Here's £100.

People

1   Match each of the following colloquial names for certain types of people with the correct description below.

a pain in the neck	a crank	a lone wolf	a dare-devil
a busybody	a sponger	a battle-axe	a slow coach
a rolling stone	a tomboy	a day-dreamer	a golden boy

(a) He's always got his head in the clouds, always fantasizing.
(b) She's very inquisitive about my private life.
(c) He loves taking dangerous risks.
(d) He can't settle down. He goes from job to job, place to place.
(e) He's always borrowing money and living off other people.
(f) She's very aggressive and bossy. She likes to dominate.
(g) Everyone thinks he'll get rapid promotion. He's destined to succeed.
(h) He's always slow and behind the others in his work or studies.
(i) She's got extremely odd, eccentric, unconventional ideas and theories.
(j) He's a real nuisance. I can't stand him.
(k) He likes to do things on his own.
(l) She's a girl who likes to play rough, boys' games.

2   Instructions as above.

a tear-away	a clock-watcher	a layabout	a miser
a wind-bag	a litter-lout	a slave-driver	a slob
a name-dropper	a road-hog	a jay-walker	a fare-dodger

(a) She talks on and on about her opinions and ideas.
(b) He keeps count of every penny he has and only spends money if he must.
(c) She likes to mention all the famous and important people she's met.

(d)   He makes his employees work extremely hard.
(e)   She crosses the road without bothering to look at the traffic.
(f)   He's lazy and prefers not to work.
(g)   She drops rubbish anywhere and never puts it in the bin.
(h)   He drives very inconsiderately of other drivers.
(i)   She's only interested in leaving work and going home.
(j)   She avoids paying when she travels on public transport.
(k)   He dresses and behaves in a very careless, often disgusting, way.
(l)   He's a bit wild, always getting into fights and other trouble.

Small Quantities

1   The following words represent small pieces or quantities. Put each
in its correct place in the sentences below. Some words must be used more
than once.

glimmer	**grain**	**fragment**
dot	**shred**	**crumb**
blade	**trace**	**speck**

(a)   She was very houseproud. There wasn't a _____ of dirt in her kitchen.
(b)   They were so hungry they ate the whole loaf of bread without letting a single _____ fall to the ground.
(c)   The desert stretched for miles. Nothing green. Not a single _____ of grass.
(d)   We watched the ship as it sailed away until it was just a _____ on the horizon.
(e)   His views are dangerous and extreme, and yet there is a _____ of truth in what he says.
(f)   The accusations against him are completely groundless. There isn't a _____ of evidence to support them.
(g)   Archaeologists are examining a _____ of a vase which they think is over 5,000 years old.
(h)   There now seems to be a _____ of hope that the strike will be averted.
(i)   The famine is so bad in that area that the people haven't seen a single _____ of rice for weeks.
(j)   One day in June 1987, he suddenly disappeared without _____ and no one has seen him since.
(k)   The police found a tiny _____ of lipstick on the wineglass.

2   Instructions as above.

hint	**clue**	**breath**
flake	**drop**	**puff**
dash	**item**	**scrap**

(a)   'Whisky?' 'Well, just a _____, please.'
(b)   Don't ask me about the economic situation. I haven't a _____.
(c)   I'm just going out for a _____ of fresh air.
(d)   I watched a rain-_____ trickling slowly down the window.
(e)   I'd like my coffee almost black please. Just a very small _____ of milk.
(f)   'What a lovely smell. What is it?' 'Some spices and I think some seafood and also just a _____ of lemon.'
(g)   I wrote the phone-number down on a _____ of paper I tore from an envelope.

(h) Everything was very still. Not a leaf moved. There wasn't the smallest _____ of wind.

(i) After a meal they always gave any _____s of left-over food to the dog.

(j) Here's an interesting _____ of news about a boy who found £500 in the street.

(k) If you put a snow-_____ under a special microscope, you will see it has a wonderful pattern.

Social Types

1   The following is a list of colloquial names for various social types, i.e. different kinds of people one meets at parties and elsewhere. Use the most suitable one to complete each description below.

wet blanket	Don Juan	gate-crasher
wallflower	chatterbox	good mixer
gossip	femme fatale	life and soul of the party
social climber		

(a) He's very lively and the centre of any group he's in. People always have a good time when he's there. He's the _____.

(b) She's so negative and boring. She has a depressing effect on any group of people she's with. She's a _____.

(c) She's confident and interested in other people. She likes to meet different kinds of people. She's a _____.

(d) He goes to parties and other occasions without an invitation. He just walks in. He's a _____.

(e) Unfortunately she is not usually asked to dance by anyone. She just stands there hoping. She's a _____.

(f) He just can't stop talking. He goes on and on excitedly, about totally unimportant things. He's a _____.

(g) He loves to discuss and pass on news or rumours about people's private lives. He's a _____.

(h) She's dangerously attractive to men. Half the men she meets fall in love with her. She's a _____.

(i) He knows he's attractive to women. They always fall for him. He's got lots of girl-friends. He's a _____.

(j) She's very conscious of her social position and is always trying to improve it by meeting 'upper-class' people. She's a _____.

2   What type or types of person from the list at the top of the exercise above ...

... would be good to have at a party?

... would you especially avoid?

... might have a lot of romantic relationships?

... makes friends easily?

... would get on well together? (make pairs, e.g. Don Juan and femme fatal)

... are you?

3   Instructions as in Exercise 1.

| parasite | good company | bore | early bird | loner |
| socialite | trouble-maker | killjoy | jet-setter | snob |

(a) He's a pleasant, interesting person to have with you at any time. He's _____.
(b) She thinks she's socially superior. She looks down on others. She's a _____.
(c) He's very strict and correct. I think he doesn't like other people to enjoy themselves. He's a _____.
(d) She's always the first to arrive at a party. If the party's due to start at seven, she's there on the dot, or earlier. She's an _____.
(e) He likes to spend a lot of time alone. He's not keen on parties and usually does things on his own. He's a _____.
(f) She goes on and on telling people about her children, her house, her job, her opinions … I could go to sleep. She's a _____.
(g) She's very rich and spends her time between grand social occasions and luxury holidays in different parts of the world. She's a _____.
(h) He's always borrowing money and asking for help from other people. He's a _____.
(i) He's an upper-class person and he's often seen at high-society parties and other social events. He's a _____.
(j) She's always causing difficulties for other people by interfering in their lives. She's a _____.

4   What type or types of person from the list at the top of Exercise 3 …
… is extroverted?
… is introverted?
… might be class-conscious?
… do you find interesting?
… would get on well together? (make pairs, e.g. socialite and snob)
… are you?

Sounds

1   Put the most suitable sound from the following list into each sentence.

| drone | gasp | yell | chant | moan |
| snort | scream | whimper | boo | cheer |

(a) I heard the _____ of a terrified woman.
(b) He gave a tired _____ of pain.
(c) The Queen's arrival was met with an enthusiastic _____ from the crowd.
(d) The referee made another unpopular decision and the crowd began to _____.
(e) When demonstrators march through the streets, they often _____ political slogans.
(f) He gave a _____ of surprise when he found the shower was ice-cold.
(g) The taxi-driver gave a _____ of contempt at the small tip.
(h) He used to _____ on and on monotonously and some of his listeners went to sleep listening to him.
(i) The little baby began to _____ weakly.
(j) I had to _____ at the top of my voice to make him hear me above the noise.

2 Which sounds from the list at the top of the exercise above …
… can express pain?
… can express disapproval?
… can express surprise?
… are loud?
… are quiet?
… are more normally associated with men?
… are more normally associated with women?
… might also be made by machines?
… are often heard at football matches?
… might be heard in a demonstration?
… might come from a theatre audience?
… can you make?

3 Instructions as in Exercise 1.

| pop | sizzle | thud | hiss | blare |
| tinkle | clink | swish | toll | chime |

(a) The great bell began to _____ sadly, solemnly, rhythmically.
(b) Some clocks _____ every hour.
(c) Tiny bells _____ in the wind.
(d) The heavy object fell to the ground with a _____.
(e) I love to hear the _____ of eggs and bacon frying in the pan.
(f) The peace and quiet was shattered when someone's radio began to _____ out.
(g) I heard a _____ from the tyre and knew I had a puncture.
(h) His sword stroke missed me by half an inch and I heard a _____ as it passed my nose.
(i) The ice-cube dropped into the empty glass with a _____.
(j) The cork finally came out of the bottle of champagne with a loud _____.

4 Which sounds from the list at the top of the exercise above …
… do you consider pleasant?   … are quiet?
… do you consider unpleasant?   … are often heard in a house?
… are made by bells?   … are often heard at a party?
… are loud?   … can you make?

5 Instructions as in Exercise 1.

| plop | boom | squelch | murmur | chirrup |
| hoot | rattle | squeak | rumble | click |

(a) I heard a _____ as he put his foot into the deep, wet mud.
(b) The small stone dropped into the water with a quiet _____.
(c) The heavy old metal cart began to _____ over the stony road.
(d) I heard a loud _____ as the cannon fired.
(e) There is no more joyous sound than the _____ of bird-song.
(f) I can hear a _____. Something in your car needs oiling.
(g) I heard the _____ of rolling thunder in the distance.
(h) There was a small _____ as he closed the car-door.
(i) The impatient motorist began to _____ at the slow car in front.
(j) From my house you can hear the gentle _____ of a stream.

6   Which sounds from the list at the top of the exercise above ...

... do you consider pleasant?
... do you consider unpleasant?
... do you associate with the town?
... do you associate with the country?
... are loud?
... are quiet?
... are made by machines?
... can describe the way people speak?
... can be made by animals or birds?
... can you make?

7   The onomatopoeic words in this exercise are usually used as nouns,
e.g. The constant *tap-tap-tap* of typewriters drove him mad.
Match each sound on the left below with an item on the right.

(a)	ding-dong	iron gates closing
(b)	tick-tock	violin-string breaking
(c)	twang	wood fire burning
(d)	clang	large bell
(e)	toot-toot	car braking at speed
(f)	bleep	car horn
(g)	bang	clock
(h)	pitter-patter	horses' hoofs on road
(i)	crackle	light rain on window
(j)	screech	bath-water going down plug-hole
(k)	clip-clop	electronic personal caller
(l)	gurgle	gun
(m)	ping	spoon tapping empty wine-glass

Space Travel

Put each of the following words and phrases in its correct space below.

orbit	**splashdown**	**astronaut**	**mission**
dock	**countdown**	**launching pad**	**gravity**
launch	**spacecraft**	**lift-off**	**manned**

The first rockets to go into space carried no living creatures, but later ones had mice or even dogs on them to see how (a) _____ (or rather the lack of it) would affect them. The first (b) _____ space-flight took place in 1962 and the first (c) _____ was the American, Alan Shepherd. Everything at the (d) _____ was checked and ready as he walked out to take his place in the rocket. Thousands of people had come to watch the (e) _____ and they were silent as the final (f) _____ began: 10, 9, 8, 7, 6, 5, 4, 3, 2, 1, zero – (g) _____! The enormous object raised itself into the sky and began its historic journey, to (h) _____ safely in the ocean four hours later. Since then great progress has been made. Alan Shepherd simply went up and came down again, but now (i) _____ can go into (j) _____ and circle the earth for days or weeks, or two of them can (k) _____ in space, enabling people to pass between them. Each (l) _____ extends man's knowledge of space.

Sport

1   Match each sport with the place where it is played - a court, a track, a course, a ring, a pool, a pitch, a circuit, a range, a rink.

(a) football
(b) swimming
(c) golf
(d) athletics
(e) tennis
(f) volley-ball
(g) basketball
(h) boxing
(i) shooting
(j) skating
(k) car-racing
(l) (horse)race

2   Match each sport on the left below with two pieces of equipment on the right.

(a) ice hockey
(b) archery
(c) golf
(d) tennis
(e) badminton
(f) boxing
(g) car-racing
(h) horse-racing
(i) cycling
(j) shooting
(k) winter sports
(l) gymnastics
(m) fencing

club/tee
racket/net
puck/stick
parallel bars/mat
saddle/handlebars
toboggan/goggles
bow/arrows
helmet/steering-wheel
épée/mask
whip/reins
racket/shuttlecock
gloves/gumshield
rifle/target

3   In what sports are the following phrases heard and what do they mean?

(a) They're off!
(b) Seconds out!
(c) Fore!
(d) It's a foul, ref!
(e) Forty – love
(f) On your marks … Get set …
(g) Three – nil
(h) A bull's-eye!
(i) Four faults.

ANIMAL AND BIRD SOUNDS

Animals and birds probably make the same sounds all over the world, but we write these sounds differently in different languages. This is how some of them appear in English.

dogs: woof-woof
cats: miaow
ducks: quack-quack
birds: tweet-tweet

donkeys: hee-haw
cockerels: cock-a-doodle-doo
cows: moo
sheep: baa

Time

1   Put each of the following words or phrases in its correct space in the sentences below.

turn of the century   **time zones**   **decade**   **era**
the small hours   **digital**   **century**   **spell**
chronological   **local time**

(a) Her parties usually finish before midnight, but sometimes they go on
      into _____.
(b) People who have _____ watches tend to say '7.50' rather than '10 to 8'.
(c) The plane is due to reach Bangkok at 5.30 a.m. _____.
(d) If you cross Russia, you pass through eight different _____.
(e) Novels don't always describe events in _____ order. It can be confusing.
(f) The First World War took place in the second _____ of this _____.
(g) After leaving university he had a _____ of teaching and then went into
      industry.
(h) In British history the period 1837 to 1901 is known as the Victorian _____.
(i) But that happened at the _____! It was more than 90 years ago!

2   Explain the difference between the items in each of the following pairs.
(a) dawn and dusk
(b) a month and a calendar month
(c) a year and a leap year

Tools and Equipment

1   Match each occupation on the left below with the most appropriate tool
or piece of equipment on the right.
(a) doctor   a rake
(b) gardener   a hose
(c) jockey   a plane
(d) chef   an axe
(e) fireman   a baton
(f) lumberjack   a stethoscope
(g) conductor   a rolling pin
(h) blacksmith   an anchor
(i) carpenter   a whip
(j) photographer   a spanner
(k) mechanic   an exposure metre
(l) sailor   an anvil

2   Instructions as above.
(a) violinist   a scalpel
(b) window cleaner   a truncheon
(c) fisherman   a pneumatic drill
(d) tailor   a bucket
(e) surgeon   a bow
(f) usherette   a tape measure
(g) policeman   a net
(h) bricklayer   a spade

(i)	hairdresser	a compass
(j)	labourer	a torch
(k)	road mender	a trowel
(l)	navigator	a drier

3 Instructions as above.

(a)	disc jockey	radar
(b)	frogman	a briefcase
(c)	businessman	a turntable
(d)	librarian	a parking meter
(e)	office cleaner	flippers
(f)	air traffic controller	scaffolding
(g)	builder	a vacuum cleaner
(h)	traffic warden	a palette
(i)	undertaker	a crane
(j)	architect	a catalogue
(k)	artist	a hearse
(l)	docker	blueprints

4 Instructions as above.

(a)	a musician	a last
(b)	drugs detective	a clapperboard
(c)	weaver	a score
(d)	football referee	a kiln
(e)	shoemaker	a drill
(f)	telephone operator	a sniffer dog
(g)	farmer	a loom
(h)	potter	a filing cabinet
(i)	secretary	a whistle
(j)	film director	a till
(k)	dentist	a plough
(l)	cashier	headphones

GOBBLEDEGOOK

When the language of government announcements, official regulations and legal English is so complex that we cannot understand it, we call it 'gobbledegook'. Here is an example.

'Regulation 4 of the Child Support Appeal Tribunal (Procedure) Regulations 1992 provides that where the Chairman of the Tribunal does not have jurisdiction to entertain a purported appeal he may make a decision to that effect and such declaration shall dispose of the purported appeal.'

Word Formation

Word Forms

Fill each space in the sentences below with the correct form of the word in bold print about it.

E.g. **decide**

(a) We must come to a _____ very soon.
(b) We beat them _____. We won 7:0.
(c) He can never make up his mind. He's very _____.

Answers:

(a) decision   (b) decisively   (c) indecisive

1   beauty

(a) She is very _____.
(b) She's training to be a _____.
(c) They're going to _____ the town with more trees and parks.

2   pay

(a) To buy this car I made a monthly _____ of £280 for two years.
(b) Please make your cheque _____ to John Watson.
(c) The person a cheque is made out to is called the _____.

3   receive

(a) She works as a _____ at a hotel in Scotland.
(b) Ask for a _____ when you buy something, in case you need to return it.
(c) I made several suggestions to improve production, but the management was not very _____ to my ideas.

4   hero

(a) He received a medal for his _____.
(b) They fought _____ in the war.
(c) She was described as a _____.

5   produce

(a) _____ of the new sports car has been halted by a strike.
(b) China is one of the world's leading _____ of rice.
(c) I'm afraid the talks were totally _____. We didn't reach agreement on anything.

6   explain

(a) An _____ leaflet is given to all purchasers of the machine.
(b) His disappearance is very strange, in fact quite _____.
(c) I think you owe me an _____ for your behaviour.

7   compare

(a) This is _____ better than that. In fact, there is really no _____.
(b) Scientists have made _____ tests on the new drugs.

8 advise

(a) Until the situation has settled down, it is _____ to travel to that country.

(b) The government set up an _____ body on the use of drugs in sport.

(c) I doubt the _____ of drinking alcohol while undergoing that medical treatment.

9 admire

(a) She was a pleasant, attractive girl, always surrounded by _____.

(b) I am full of _____ for what she has achieved.

(c) I approve of him wholeheartedly. He is an _____ man.

10 stable

(a) To _____ the boat in rough sea, we redistributed the weight.

(b) Between 1860 and 1900 the country had a number of revolutions and uprisings. It was a time of great _____.

(c) The exchange rate is going up and down dramatically. It's very _____ at the moment.

11 economy

(a) We're spending too much. We must _____.

(b) This car uses a lot of petrol. It's terribly _____.

(c) The Chancellor (Minister of Finance) is responsible for _____ affairs.

12 reside

(a) This is the President's official _____.

(b) There's no industry or entertainment here. It's a _____ district.

(c) All _____ of the neighbouring houses were warned of the gas leak.

13 comfort

(a) In that tense situation I found the good news very _____.

(b) I felt rather _____, so I put a soft cushion behind me.

(c) She sat in terrible _____ on the hard chair for over an hour.

14 dead

(a) The increasing number of _____ in traffic accidents is alarming.

(b) Be careful! That's a _____ poison!

(c) The doctor gave him an injection to _____ the pain.

15 demonstrate

(a) The _____ marched through the streets chanting slogans.

(b) Grandfather rarely showed the affection he felt for his family. He was a very _____ person.

(c) What you say is _____ false. Let me show you the facts.

16 imitate

(a) The bag is made of _____ leather.

(b) Small children are very _____ in their behaviour. They just copy what they see.

(c) His acting style is _____. No one can copy him.

17 argue

(a) She had an _____ with her husband last night.

(b) He's a very bad-tempered, _____ chap. He's always quarrelling.

(c) She is _____ the finest pianist in the world.

18 repeat
(a) He lost his temper and used disgusting, _____ language.
(b) In this essay you've said the same thing several times. It's very _____.
(c) I hope there will be no _____ of this shocking behaviour.

19 fail
(a) She is very efficient, and _____ polite to the customers.
(b) He considered himself a _____. He had succeeded in nothing.
(c) It was difficult to see much in the _____ light.

20 courage
(a) His friends tried to _____ him from attempting the dangerous climb.
(b) She _____ stood in the way of the escaping robbers.
(c) His parents gave him a lot of _____ in his studies.

21 real
(a) I think it's a bit _____ to hope that world peace can be gained so easily.
(b) He spends all his time in romantic daydreams. He's lost touch with _____.
(c) Ladies and gentlemen, I am a _____ and I think we must face facts.

22 false
(a) She was accused of _____ the financial accounts.
(b) It is a _____ to say he did it when you know he didn't.
(c) The _____ of his argument was obvious to everyone.

23 prophesy
(a) I am not a _____ and I would not like to make a _____ on whether the world can survive this age of nuclear weapons.
(b) What he wrote in 1930 was _____. Much of what he described has come true.

24 describe
(a) The damage caused by the earthquake cannot be imagined. It was _____.
(b) The teacher asked them to write a _____ passage about their home towns.
(c) The witness was able to give a full _____ of the wanted man.

25 friend
(a) The _____ between the two soon developed into love.
(b) In London she was _____ by a rich woman who looked after her and helped her.
(c) The desert is a dangerous, _____ place.

26 sense
(a) He felt a strange, painful _____ in his back.
(b) Even the most _____ person ought to appreciate the beauty of this music.
(c) What an idiotic, _____ thing to do!

27 famous
(a) The _____ of the Beatles soon spread outside Britain.
(b) The day of the massacre will go down in history as a terrible, _____ day. It was a day of _____.

28 defend

(a) I just want to ask you a few ordinary questions, so why don't you relax? Why are you so _____?
(b) The government's policy on arms is shocking. It is quite _____.
(c) We must do all we can for the _____ of this nation against possible attack.

29 agree

(a) What an unpleasant, _____ old woman she is!
(b) We finally reached _____ on the matter at midnight.
(c) I liked the place. I found the people, the weather and the food very _____.

30 possess

(a) In his will he left all his money and _____ to his wife.
(b) She was a very _____ mother. She gave her son very little freedom.
(c) The actor playing the main part should be the _____ of a very good voice, good looks and a very strong physique.

31 different

(a) I'm afraid I have to _____. I don't agree with you at all.
(b) Politeness is one thing. Real kindness is another. You must learn to _____ between the two.
(c) We get along pretty well, although of course we have our _____ from time to time.

32 active

(a) The strike was organised by a group of political _____.
(b) The fire-prevention system is _____ by any small increase in temperature.
(c) It is quite safe to go near the volcano. It has been _____ for years.

33 form

(a) It is especially important for children to have love and affection in their _____ years.
(b) The slight _____ in his left hand was corrected by surgery.
(c) The police are considering the _____ of a new anti-drugs unit.

34 compel

(a) Military service is no longer _____ in South Africa.
(b) Membership of the Students' Club is entirely voluntary. There is no _____ whatsoever.
(c) All staff should attend the meeting. Only the most _____ reasons for absence will be accepted.

35 create

(a) Ian Fleming, the _____ of James Bond, died in 1964.
(b) Although she is very able technically, she isn't _____ enough for this kind of work.
(c) The _____ of the North Atlantic Treaty Organisation took place in 1949.

36 enthusiasm

(a) They threw themselves _____ into the new project.
(b) He's a real golf _____. He loves the game.
(c) They didn't really _____ over my idea. In fact there was some opposition.

37 necessary

(a) We regret that the present economic difficulties will _____ a reduction in our work force.

(b) I sympathise with his point of view, but I don't always _____ agree with him.

(c) He lives very simply, with just the basic _____ of life.

38 destroy

(a) The control centre is deep underground and completely _____ except by a direct hit from a nuclear missile.

(b) War plans include the immediate _____ of all enemy military bases.

(c) His criticism of my work was entirely _____. There was nothing useful or constructive in it at all.

39 manage

(a) Talks between workers and _____ have broken down and a strike now seems unavoidable.

(b) The boy was very violent and his parents found him _____.

(c) To improve his qualifications he's taking a course in _____ skills.

40 believe

(a) It was an incredible story, quite _____.

(b) She is a person of very strong religious _____.

(c) His explanation was obviously false and the judge made no attempt to hide his _____.

PORTMANTEAU WORDS

New expressions are often created by combining parts of two words. 'Smog' is a combination of 'smoke' and 'fog'. A film about someone's life is sometimes callled a 'biopic' (biographical picture). A 'bedsit' is a room which serves as both a bedroom and sitting room. These combinations are called 'portmanteau' words. Can you explain the folowing?

Swatch	brunch	motel	Oxfam
hazchem	Oxbridge	Interpol	Eurovision
Chunnel	camcorder	guesstimate	fanzine
vegeburger	shopaholic	ScotRail	ecotastrophe
fantabulous	ginormous	Amex	docudrama

Prefixes

1   **arch-** (chief, main, highest-ranking) **out-** (more, better etc. than)
mal- (badly, wrongly) **pseudo-** (false, pretended).
Put each of the above prefixes in its correct space in the sentences below.
(a)   In my opinion this book is just _____-intellectual rubbish.
(b)   Although he was older than his wife, he _____ lived her by ten years.
(c)   Priests are not often ambitious men, but he had set his heart on becoming
_____ bishop.
(d)   The launch of the space-rocket was delayed by a _____ function in the fuel
system.
(e)   At the beginning of the nineteenth century, Britain's _____-enemy was France.
(f)   He completely _____ boxed his opponent and knocked him out in the
seventh round.
(g)   Children who grow up in time of war are more likely to be _____ adjusted
than other children.
(h)   He uses _____-scientific language to persuade his readers.
(i)   These squalid, dark, cramped, _____ odorous rooms are homes to whole
families of people.
(j)   She was the finest dancer in the country. She _____ shone all the others.

2   **Explain the meanings of the following words and phrases.**
a)   a pseudonym   e)   malnutrition
b)   arch-rivals   f)   pseudo-religious
c)   maladministration   g)   an arch-villain
d)   out-size clothes   h)   to outstay your welcome

3   **a-** (not, without) **hyper-** (extremely, too) **fore-** (before, in front of)
neo- (new, revived)
(a)   The museum was built in the middle of the last century in the _____-classical
style popular at that time.
(b)   Who can _____ tell what the future holds for us?
(c)   It's no use asking him about the political system or the parties. He doesn't know
or care. He's completely _____ political.
(d)   It's quite normal to complain if you think something is wrong, but I do feel that
you are sometimes _____ critical.
(e)   The authorities are concerned at the activities of a small _____- Nazi
movement.
(f)   You must be very careful what you say about her poems. She's a _____
sensitive person.
(g)   She didn't know the difference between right and wrong. She had no
conscience at all. She was simply _____ moral.
(h)   The police claimed that she had some _____ knowledge of the murder
attempt and could have prevented it.
(i)   He was standing in the middle, in the _____ ground of the picture.
(j)   Young children can sometimes be _____ active, which means that they can't
keep still.

4 Explain the meanings of the following words and phrases.

(a) neo-imperialism
(e) hypertension
(b) an atheist
(f) a foregone conclusion
(c) a foretaste
(g) an asymmetrical shape
(d) a hypermarket
(h) a neo-Fascist

5 **uni-, mono-** (one) **duo-, bi-** (two) **tri-** (three) **quad-, quart-** (four)
pent-, quin- (five) **sex-** (six) **sept-** (seven) **oct-** (eight) **non-** (nine)
dec- (ten) **cent-** (hundred)
Complete the words in the passage below.

George Willis was born in 1900 and was too young to go into uni_____ in the
First World War, which took place in the second dec_____ of the cent_____.
Instead he finished his schooling and went to university. Like most Oxford colleges,
his college was built round a quad _____ and a photograph of him there shows
him wearing a mono _____ in his eye, one of his many eccentricities. He rode a
tri_____, declaring it to be safer and more stable than a bi_____. His subject
was zoology. Initially he studied bi_____, but soon tired of two-legged creatures
and took an interest in quad _____, developing a special affection for elephants.
However, all animal life fascinated him and he was often to be seen in the
Oxfordshire countryside, observing wildlife through his bi_____ or setting up his
tri_____ to record it in photographs. Marine creatures also attracted him,
especially, for some reason, the oct_____. He was also creative in such diverse
fields as engineering (he proposed a scheme for mono_____ transport in London)
and music (he formed a jazz sex_____, which later became a quin_____ when
the drummer joined the navy, a quart_____ when the violinist was run over by a
bus and a tri_____ when the trombonist was imprisoned for bi_____). He
travelled widely and spoke French so well that he was completely bi_____. He was
a fine sportsman and won many prizes in the pent_____. In 1972, although by
this time a sept_____, he wrote his first play, a strange piece which consisted of a
duo_____ between Shakespeare and Churchill. He is still active and talkative,
although conversations with him tend to be mono_____. He talks and others
listen. Always optimistic, he looks forward to continuing his busy life as a
non_____ and to becoming a cent_____. He lives with his wife, a lively
oct_____, and has two sons and a daughter, whose birth as tri_____ in 1927 he
describes as the happiest event in his eventful life.

6 Explain the meanings of the following words.

a) bicentenary
f) decathlon
k) biplane
b) pentagon
g) sexagenarian
l) bicameral
c) centenary
h) quintuplets
m) unicycle
d) tricolour
i) bisect
n) quadruplets
e) monotonous
j) cent
o) unicorn

Suffixes

1 **-phobia** (fear or hatred of) **-cide** (killer, killing) **-gamy** (marriage)

Put each of the above suffixes in its correct place in the sentences below.

(a) Those rose-bushes need protection. Spray them with insecti_____.

(b) He gets very tense and nervous in enclosed spaces like lifts and the underground. He suffers from claustro_____.

(c) The custom of having more than one wife or husband is known as 'poly_____

(d) Some people, and some animals, are terrified of water. This aversion is known as aqua_____.

(e) His problems overwhelmed him and he finally committed sui_____.

(f) When he was arrested and charged with bi_____, both his wives stood by him.

(g) His Anglo-_____ comes from some bad experiences he had in England.

(h) Following the man's death, his wife was charged with homi_____.

2 Explain the meanings of the following words and phrases.

a) germicide   d) a monogamous society

b) xenophobia   e) fratricide

c) patricide   f) agoraphobia

3 **-maniac** (obsessed person) **-phile** (lover of) **-monger** (dealer in)

Put each of the above suffixes in its correct place in the sentences below.

(a) A person who makes and exploits war is called a war _____.

(b) He has always been a biblio_____ and has amassed a vast collection of books over the years.

(c) He has a shop selling pots and pans, tools and other metal goods. He's an iron_____.

(d) He's unbelievably self-centred and arrogant. He's a complete ego_____.

(e) She loved the year she spent in Italy and has been an Italo_____ ever since.

(f) Some journalists are perfectly honest and well-meaning but she just makes a profit from gossip and rumour. She's just a cheap scandal _____.

(g) A klepto_____ is a person who has a compulsive desire to steal.

(h) His fondness for drink became an addiction, and his doctor says he is now a dipso_____.

4 Explain the meanings of the following words and phrases.

a) a pyromaniac   c) an anglophile   e) a fishmonger

b) Francophilia   d) a mania   f) a film maniac

5 **-worthy** (deserving, fit for) **-like** (similar to) **-most** (furthest)

Put each of the above suffixes in its correct place in the sentences below.

(a) To me, at 14, the film-stars I saw at my local cinema were god_____ creatures.

(b) John O'Groats in Scotland is the northern_____ town in mainland Britain.

(c) We are pleased to present you with this award for your praise_____ work among the poor of this city.

(d) In the old days it was not considered lady _____ for a woman to smoke in public, if at all.

(e) Architecture during that period was very boring. Almost every building was a box-_____ structure, with no variation or decoration to please the eye.

(f) We're looking for an honest, reliable, trust_____ person to handle our legal affairs.

(g) He betrayed the inner _____ secrets of his country's government to the enemy.

(h) A small accident like that won't appear in the papers. It isn't news _____ enough.

6 Explain the meanings of the following phrases.
(a) a business-like manner
(b) his foremost thought
(c) a roadworthy car
(d) a noteworthy comment
(e) a life-like statue
(f) outermost defences

7 **-wards** (in the direction of) **-esque** (like, in the manner of)
-some (causing, making)
Put each of the above suffixes in its correct place in the sentences below.
(a) I have a backache which is a bit trouble_____ at times.
(b) He cast his eyes heaven_____ as if imploring God for help or pity.
(c) It's very pictur_____ here, with the trees attractively framing the view of the river.
(d) From Colombia we went south_____ through Ecuador, Peru and Bolivia to Argentina.
(e) Man's first view of the earth from space was an awe_____ sight.
(f) The back garden faces sea_____ so you can always be sure of a pleasant view.
(g) I'm afraid I find her constant chatter gets a bit weari_____ after a while.
(h) The architecture here is rather Roman_____. Look at the round arches and thick walls.

8 Explain the meanings of the following phrases.
(a) quarrelsome boys
(b) outwardly confident
(c) a statuesque figure
(d) a downward movement
(e) a tiresome person
(f) a Kafkaesque novel

9 **-scape** (scenery) **-scope** (means of observing) **-let, -ette, -ling** (small)
Put each of the above suffixes in its correct place in the sentences below.
(a) Even the most powerful tele _____ does not make the smallest stars visible.
(b) I watched a drop_____ of rain move slowly down the window.
(c) His most famous sea_____ was painted in 1879 and hangs in the National Gallery.
(d) A gos_____ is a young goose.
(e) The award takes the form of a silver statu_____ of the Greek god, Adonis.
(f) The first television picture of the hitherto mysterious moon_____ was the most dramatic sight I have ever seen.
(g) His home is in the country and he's wondering if he can afford to buy a flat_____ in London too.
(h) The crew of a submarine just below the surface can see what is happening above by looking through the peri_____.
(i) Travelling by car, you have the chance to stop in the countryside to admire the land_____.

10 Explain the meanings of the following words and phrases.
a) a microscopic insect
b) a piglet
c) a duckling
d) a kitchenette
e) a marvellous cloudscape
f) a booklet

11   -ist

What are the following people?

(a)   An ornithologist
(b)   A philatelist
(c)   A feminist
(d)   A numismatist
(e)   A philanthropist
(f)   A pathologist
(g)   A linguist

(h)   A dramatist
(i)   A seismologist
(j)   A manicurist
(k)   A pharmacist
(l)   A meteorologist
(m) An arsonist
(n)   A taxidermist

(o)   A misogynist
(p   A somnambulist
(q)   A sinologist
(r)   A chiropodist
(s)   A graphologist

Compound Adjectives

Rewrite each of the sentences below, forming a compound adjective from the two words in italics and making any other changes necessary.

E.g.   The journey took *ten hours.*
          They *make* these chocolates by *hand.*
          Her hat *caught* everyone's *eye.*
          The doctor was *trained* in *Germany.*
          The memory was both *bitter* and *sweet.*

Answers: It was a *ten-hour* journey.
          These chocolates are *hand-made.*
          She wore an *eye-catching* hat.
          He's a *German-trained* doctor.
          It was a *bitter-sweet* memory.

1
(a)   That thing *looks dangerous.*
(b)   Mr Reed is an accountant who was *born* in *London.*
(c)   She always *dresses* very *smartly.*
(d)   It was painted *red* like the colour of *bricks.*
(e)   She had eyes *like a cat.*
(f)   It was an occasion which was *happy* and *sad* at the same time.
(g)   The tower has a *shape* like a *mushroom.*
(h)   He was *famous* all over the *world.*
(i)   We had to write a composition of *200 words.*

2
(a)   The meal *tasted awful.*
(b)   Only planes with a *single engine* can land here.
(c)   A building of *five storeys* suddenly collapsed.
(d)   We walked along a corridor which had a *red carpet.*
(e)   This machine is *operated* by *hand.*
(f)   The new director is an economist *educated* at *Oxford.*
(g)   He has very *broad shoulders.*
(h)   She's always very *satisfied* with *herself.*
(i)   My sister is very *conscious* of *dress.*

3

(a) We'll have a guide who *speaks French.*
(b) The walls were as *blue* as the *sky*.
(c) I looked at the sea, which was rather *blue* but also rather *green.*
(d) The ship sailed with a crew of *eight men.*
(e) She had *fair hair.*
(f) The new machinery, *built* in *America*, will arrive next month.
(g) I heard a voice that *sounded strange.*
(h) These tigers *eat men.*
(i) He always has a *bad temper.*

4

(a) The experiment was done with balloons *filled* with *gas.*
(b) My teenage son is *mad* about *football.*
(c)   I'm afraid my wife *spends* very *freely.*
(d) He certainly has *good intentions*.
(e) They have very *bad manners.*
(f) The firm has its *base* in *New York.*
(g) Those cars are a very *high price.*
(h) The noise *split* our *ears!*
(i) I need a car with *four doors.*

Noun Plurals

1   Put the words in brackets into the sentences, in the correct order, in their plural forms.
(a) A large number of _____ fled in fear when a flock of _____ suddenly landed within a few _____ of them. (mouse, foot, goose)
(b) Automobile _____ have all too many _____ to tell of _____ in deliveries of the special security _____ and are considering ways of manufacturing their own. (key, company, delay, story)
(c) Security _____ believe the _____ climbed along the _____ of several houses before forcing open an upper window of the office building with _____ and escaping with the contents of two _____. (safe, chief, knife, thief, roof)
(d) With the help of old _____, war-time Paris was recreated in the film _____ for the film '_____ of War', in which all the _____ were played by unknown actors. (echo, studio, hero, photo)
(e) _____ were surprised when no fewer than six _____ in full uniform, carrying _____, arrived in _____ to attend a series of _____. (court-martial, brief-case, passer-by, commander-in-chief, police car)
(f) The farmer's _____ and some wild _____ were sometimes alarmed by low-flying _____. (deer, aircraft, sheep)

2   Write these words in their plural forms.
(a) crisis
(b) chateau
(c) memorandum
(d) analysis
(e) bureau
(f) stratum
(g) thesis
(h) phenomenon
(i) criterion
(j) medium

Problem Words

Confusing Word Pairs

Choose the correct word for each space.

1   **misused** (badly, wrongly used)
    disused (no longer used)

(a) An airport _____ since its closure ten years before was used for car-racing.
(b) They complained that the new law had been _____ to suppress individual liberties.
(c) Be careful of this word. It is often _____ .
(d) The goods were stored in a _____ cinema.

2   **unreadable** (too boring or too badly written to read)
    illegible (physically impossible to read)

(a) His hand-writing is so bad it's _____ .
(b) The book is long, uninteresting and not very well-written. I find it _____ .
(c) After years of being exposed to the sun and rain, the sign over the shop had become completely _____ .
(d) I think her novels are _____ . The style is awful and the plots are ridiculous.

3   **dependent** (depending)
    dependant (person who depends on another for home, money, food)

(a) The signing of the contract is _____ on whether you can guarantee delivery of the goods within three months.
(b) You are entitled to receive a government allowance for each _____ who is living with you.
(c) This residence document permits you, but no _____ , to live and work in this country.
(d) The empire consisted of the kingdom and all its _____ colonies.

4   **historic** (important in history)
    historical (concerning history)

(a) At the meeting of our local _____ society there will be a talk on 'France in the 19th Century'.
(b) Today we have gained our independence and our liberty. It is a _____ day for our country.
(c) She likes _____ novels, especially romances set in the 16th and 17th centuries.
(d) In 1945 there was a _____ meeting of world leaders which changed the course of world events.

5   **immigration** (coming into a country to settle)
    emigration (leaving a country to settle elsewhere)

(a) If we don't restrict _____ into this country, the pressure on our social services will be intolerable.
(b) When times were hard in Britain, there was very large _____ to Australia and Canada.

6 **dissatisfied** (discontented, displeased, not satisfied with quality)
   unsatisfied (unfulfilled, not satisfied with quantity)

(a) He ate a meal large enough for three normal people but his appetite was still _____ .

(b) I'm very _____ with this computer. It keeps breaking down.

(c) If you are _____ with the service, you should complain.

(d) Demand for the new car is still _____ in spite of an increase in production.

7 **suit** (be suitable for)
   suite (swi:t) (group of things belonging together, set)

(a) Will seven o'clock _____ you or shall I come later?

(b) She took a _____ of rooms at the Bristol Hotel.

(c) For the living-room we can either buy a complete _____ of matching furniture or get different items separately.

(d) Do you think a dark brown overcoat would _____ me?

8 **prophecy** (prediction, *noun*)
   prophesy (predict, *verb*)

(a) I _____ that he will pass his exam and get a good job.

(b) I will make a _____ . There will be a new government in less than a year.

9 **device** (new invention, means of doing something, *noun*)
   devise (invent, *verb*)

(a) Anyone who can _____ a means of recording television programmes without recording the advertisements will make a fortune.

(b) He invented a _____ for warning pilots if there was bad weather ahead.

(c) A _____ can be attached to a private telephone which keeps a record of all calls made and their cost.

(d) He managed to _____ a system of bonus payments to encourage hard-working staff.

10 **enquiry/enquiries** (request for information)
   inquiry/inquiries (formal investigation)

(a) You should make _____ at the office.

(b) Official _____ are always held after plane crashes.

(c) We have received a number of _____ about our new product since putting an advertisement in the newspaper.

(d) It was never discovered where the missing money went, in spite of a searching _____ by the bank.

11 **exhausting** (very tiring)
   exhaustive (very thorough, complete)

(a) _____ tests were carried out to discover the cause of the plane's engine failure.

(b) The older members of the group found the long journey quite _____ .

(c) He never stops talking. He's an _____ person to be with.

(d) The police carried out an _____ investigation, but the missing woman was never found.

12 **disinterested** (impartial)
uninterested (not interested, bored, apathetic)

(a) Only 22% of the people voted. The rest were totally _____ .
(b) The management and the union asked a completely _____ party to mediate between them.
(c) I don't know why he didn't go to the exhibition. Perhaps he was too busy or just _____ .
(d) France's intervention in the dispute was not entirely _____ . It gave her increased power and influence in the area.

13 **council** (district government)
counsel (i: kind of lawyer in court ii: to advise)

(a) The job of a Vocational Guidance Officer is to _____ young people on their careers.
(b) I have complained to the local _____ about the poor condition of the pavements.
(c) The prosecuting _____ demanded the death penalty but the judge gave her a life sentence.
(d) Some men from the _____ came to plant trees along the river.

14 **councillor** (member of a council)
counsellor (adviser)

(a) She and her husband often argued, so they went to a marriage _____ for help.
(b) He's always been interested in local government. Now he's been elected _____ .

15 **unknown** (not known)
infamous (shameful, notorious)

(a) The show was such a success that she went from being an _____ actress to a star overnight.
(b) Joseph Jackson was an _____ mass-murderer of Victorian times.
(c) His action in cheating poor, sick and elderly people of their savings was described by the judge as _____ .
(d) The firm was almost _____ ten years ago but now it is famous for its high-quality products.

16 **certainly** (definitely, really)
surely (expresses surprise, doubt, relief)

(a) _____ you aren't going out like that, are you?
(b) I am _____ not inviting Teresa to my party. I've never liked her.
(c) Your coat must be here somewhere, _____ !
(d) He _____ impressed me. I thought he was very bright and talented.

17 **dairy** (i: place where milk is kept, butter, cheese etc. made; shop selling milk products ii: related to milk products)
diary (daily record of events)

(a) He kept a _____ from the age of 15 to 21.
(b) We're still waiting for milk deliveries from the _____ .
(c) No, we don't grow wheat or vegetables. It's a _____ farm. We have about 200 cows.
(d) She has a regular column in the Daily News describing the various activities of the day. It's called 'Annabel's _____ .'

18 **compliment** (to praise, piece of praise)
   complement (go together or combine well, add to)
(a) He lacks confidence and she is a strong person.
    They _____ each other very well.
(b) He paid her a nice _____ on her new dress.
(c) I'd like to _____ you on your performance. It was excellent.
(d) Weight-lifting gives strength. Running increases stamina.
    The two exercises _____ each other.

19 **first** (first item in list of reasons, actions etc.)
   at first (initial attitude before change)
(a) _____ boil the water, then add salt, then put in the potatoes, then …
(b) He found the job difficult _____ , but soon got used to it.
(c) _____ they didn't like their new boss.
(d) _____ I phoned the police, then I made a list of what had been stolen, then I
    made myself a cup of tea.

20 **lastly** (final item in list of reasons, actions etc.)
   at last (final result)
(a) The police questioned him for three hours until _____ he confessed.
(b) … then stir the mixture in the saucepan, then leave for five minutes and
    _____ add sugar.
(c) _____ I succeeded in making him understand!
(d) There are several reasons why he's leaving the country. First, he hates the
    weather here, secondly, he can't find a good job, and _____ , he's homesick.

EPONYMOUS WORDS

A keen gambler in the 18th century, not wanting to leave his card game when
he wanted to have a meal, told a servant to bring him some meat between
two pieces of bread. He was the Earl of Sandwich and his name is still used for
the snack he invented. The Duke of Wellington wore high rubber boots, which
are still called 'wellingtons' (or 'wellies'). What do you know about these
famous people, all of whose names have become common words?

Captain Boycott	**Louis Braille**
Dr Guillotin	**Charles Macintosh**
Vidkun Quisling	**Mikhail Kalashnikov**
Etienne de Silhouette	**James Watt**
Marquis de Sade	**Earl of Cardigan**
Lázló Biro	**Count Alessandro Volta**

Difficult Verb Pairs

A small number of verbs give problems because the past tense (and usually also the past participle) of one verb has the same spelling as the present tense and infinitive of another. In each sentence below use the right form of the correct verb.

1   **fall, fell, fallen**
    fell, felled, felled (cut down)
(a) Prices have _____ steeply since last August.
(b) Three old trees will have to be _____ because they are diseased and dangerous.
(c) He lost his balance and _____ heavily.

2   **find, found, found**
    found, founded, founded (establish)
(a) My grandfather _____ this firm in 1924.
(b) While clearing out the bedroom, I _____ these old letters.
(c) The United Nations was _____ in 1945.

3   **bind, bound, bound** (tie up)
    bound, bounded, bounded (i: jump ii: border)
(a) Switzerland is _____ by France, Germany, Austria and Italy.
(b) The lion _____ forward and sprang at her.
(c) He was _____ hand and foot by the robbers.

4   **see, saw, seen**
    saw, sawed, sawed/sawn (cut with a saw)
(a) I suddenly _____ a face at the window.
(b) He _____ the branch in half and put the pieces on the fire.
(c) Two prisoners _____ through the bars of their cell window and escaped.

5   **grind, ground, ground** (crush into powder)
    ground, grounded, grounded (compel to remain on the ground)
(a) The ship went too near the coast and was _____ on rocks.
(b) The beans are _____ in this machine before they are put in the coffee pot.
(c) The airline has decided to _____ all its planes until special safety checks have been carried out.

6   **wind, wound** [waʊnd], **wound** (twist)
    wound [wuːnd], **wounded, wounded** (injure)
(a) The train _____ its way up the hillside and stopped just below the top.
(b) The police opened fire and _____ six of the rioters.
(c) Keep still and I'll _____ a bandage round your arm.

7   **lie, lay, lain** (be or put oneself in a horizontal position, *intransitive*)
    lay, laid, laid (put, *transitive*)
(a) He _____ the enormous box on the ground and looked for a taxi.
(b) He _____ there for an hour until someone finally heard his cries for help.
(c) In this school emphasis is _____ on discipline and hard work.
(d) I'm tired. I think I'll _____ down for a while.
(e) They were ordered to _____ down their weapons.
(f) The villages _____ at the foot of the mountains.

Some verbs have two past participle forms and there is usually no difference between the two (e.g. learned/learnt, sawed/sawn). However, in a few cases the two forms are used for two different applications of the verb and are not interchangeable. In each sentence below use the correct past participle form of the verb.

8 **bear, bore,**   **born** (give birth to)
                                  borne (i: carry ii: endure)

(a) He was _____ in Tokyo in 1906.
(b) The winning team were _____ through the streets on the shoulders of their excited supporters.
(c) No one else could have _____ the terrible experiences he went through.

9 **cost,**   **cost,**   **cost** (be of certain price)
                 costed,   **costed** (calculate the cost of)

(a) Accountants and engineers have _____ a new heating system for the factory. The board of directors will consider their estimates and decide whether to go ahead with the scheme.
(b) Houses have never _____ more than they do today.
(c) The proposed new road system has been _____ by experts at £73,000,000.

10 **hang,**   **hung,**   **hung** (suspend)
                  hanged,   **hanged** (kill by hanging)

(a) When you've _____ your coat up, come and sit down.
(b) Before the abolition of the death penalty, convicted murderers were sometimes _____ .
(c) This picture has been badly _____ . It should be nearer the light and lower.

11 **strike, struck,**   **struck** (hit)
                             stricken (attack, e.g. with fear, doubt, disease)

(a) Thousands of people have been _____ by this terrible illness.
(b) I have never _____ anyone in my life.
(c) Panic-_____ , they rushed through the flames to the exits.

AUSTRALIAN SLANG

Australian English is most interesting for its colourful slang. Many words end in '-i', '-ie', '-y' or in '-o':

uni (university)   **prezzie** (present)
postie (postman)   **barbie** (barbecue)
truckie (truck driver)   **Crissy** (Christmas)
arvo (afternoon)   **smoko** (break for cigarette and refreshment)

Other common slang expressions:

chunder (vomit), **pom, pommy** (British person), **crook** (no good, sick), **beanie** (woollen skull cap), **roo** (kangaroo)

Ambiguous Words

The following sentences have two different meanings, due to the ambiguity of the words in italics. Explain the two meanings of each sentence.

(a) She was driving on the *right* side of the road.
(b) He's very *fair*.
(c) She was a very *funny* girl.
(d) Half the workers in the factory are *idle*.
(e) They did not *recognise* the new President.
(f) She's a very *curious* person.
(g) It's a very *cheap* newspaper.
(h) They are *expected* to arrive at seven.
(i) My grandfather was a very *powerful* man.
(j) I thought he was rather *suspicious*.
(k) She was very *jealous* of her husband's reputation.
(l) She likes to *entertain* people.
(m) John *should* know the answer.
(n) He didn't *appeal* to me.
(o) The *Morning News* is a *popular* newspaper.
(p) He *might* have phoned.
(q) I'm afraid I'm not *prepared* to leave yet.
(r) The teacher *insisted* that his pupils did their homework regularly.
(s) He took *advantage* of his friend's knowledge.

False Friends

Speakers of other, mainly European, languages may come across certain English words and because they look similar to words in their own language wrongly assume that the meaning is the same. The confusion might be because of a chance similarity in spelling; because the original meaning, in one or other language, has changed over the years; or because the original word was borrowed from one language and, from the start, used differently in the other. Such words are called 'false friends'.

In each pair of words below, the first word is the false friend and the second is the word it is often confused with. Put each word in its correct place in the sentences which follow each pair.

1 **actual** (real)
   present (current, existing now)
(a) Carter and Bush are former American Presidents. Who is the _____ one?
(b) I've known many rich men, but he is the only _____ millionaire I've met.
(c) She used to work in advertising, but her _____ job is in journalism.

2 **ignore** (deliberately take no notice of, pay no attention to)
   not know
(a) His speech was interrupted by loud shouts but he wisely decided to _____ them and carry on.
(b) How can you _____ your teacher's name? You see her every day!
(c) Well, if you _____ my warnings, I cannot be responsible for what happens to you.

3   **formidable** (causing fear, difficult to achieve)
     wonderful
(a) It was a _____ party. We all enjoyed ourselves very much.
(b) To prepare for that difficult exam in only three months! That's a _____ task! I
     don't think I can do it.
(c) The northern approaches to the city are protected by _____ defences which
     only the strongest attack could penetrate.
(d) She's a _____ person. Everyone likes and admires her.

4   **camping** (activity of holidaying in a tent)
     camp-site (place for setting up tents)
(a) I like to go _____ in the summer.
(b) We found a lovely _____ near the sea to put up our tent.

5   **morale** (spirits, state of mind)
     moral (right, proper, virtuous)
(a) Regular mail and good food are important to maintain the _____ of soldiers
     during a war.
(b) 'It was a good move financially, but from the _____ point of view I have my
     doubts.
(c) As we became aware of the difficulties that lay ahead, our _____ dropped.
(d) He's a very _____ person who is guided by the highest principles.

6   **frequent** (go to often)
     attend (go to a school or course etc., be present at)
(a) Please state the name and address of the college you _____ .
(b) Criminals are known to _____ the clubs and bars in this street.
(c) Wild animals _____ the river bank at night and traps are set to catch them.
(d) Delegates from twelve countries are expected to _____ the meeting.

7   **adequate** (enough, sufficient)
     suitable (right for the purpose)
(a) Make sure you have _____ money for the trip. 10,000 pesetas should be
     enough.
(b) I'll come at six, or any other _____ time you suggest.
(c) Do you think this dress is _____ for tonight's party, or is it too formal?
(d) Rice-growing can only be successful if there is _____ rainfall.

8   **argument** (i: disagreement ii: supporting reason)
     subject (something talked or written about or studied)
(a) My favourite _____ at school was geography.
(b) He and his wife had a heated _____ about which car to buy.
(c) The best _____ against smoking is its effect on health.
(d) The _____ of the essay we had to write was 'World Peace'.

9   **eventually** (finally, after a long time)
     possibly (perhaps or maybe)
(a) The Socialist Party will win, _____ with a majority of over fifty.
(b) After travelling all day, they _____ reached home at midnight.
(c) He's arriving on Tuesday, or _____ Wednesday.
(d) At the moment he has only one shop, but he hopes to have a nationwide
     chain _____ .

10 **dancing** (activity of dance)
    dance-hall (large room where people go to dance)
(a) _____ is good exercise.
(b) We went to a nice _____ in the town.

11 **experience** (i: previous knowledge or work ii: event)
    experiment (test carried out to see result)
(a) Meeting the President was an _____ I shall never forget.
(b) We'll try an _____ with these chemicals and see what happens.
(c) This is a very responsible job, so we want someone with a lot of _____ .
(d) The _____ of arranging the students' chairs in a semi-circle was very
     successful.

12 **fabricate** (invent, make up something false)
    manufacture (make, produce in a factory)
(a) To avoid suspicion, he decided to _____ a completely false story.
(b) This is the factory where they _____ the new sports-car.
(c) Any attempt to _____ evidence will be dealt with most severely by the courts.
(d) Plans are in progress to _____ electrical appliances here, which will create
     much-needed jobs.

13 **chauffeur** (uniformed car-driver employed to drive others)
    driver (person who drives a car, lorry, bus etc.)
(a) The police stopped every vehicle on the motorway and asked the _____
     to show his or her licence.
(b) She had her own Rolls Royce and her own _____ to drive her wherever she
     wanted to go.
(c) He works as a _____ , driving ministers and civil servants from place to place.
(d) Any _____ about to stop, slow down or turn should clearly indicate his or her
     intentions to following vehicles.

14 **assist** (help)
    attend (be present at)
(a) We hope a large number of people will _____ the conference next week.
(b) The police called for members of the public to _____ in the investigation.
(c) Due to a previous engagement, the Foreign Minister will be unable to _____
     the meeting. A deputy will go instead.
(d) Lifeboats were sent out to _____ the ship in difficulties.

15 **pass** (be successful in test, exam)
    take (attempt test, exam)
(a) If I _____ the exam, I'll celebrate by giving a party.
(b) I hope you're successful in the exam. When do you _____ it?
(c) I _____ my driving test tomorrow. I hope I _____ it.

16 **remark** (say, make a comment)
    notice (happen to see)
(a) He enjoyed his stay with us, but he did _____ that he hadn't slept well.
(b) I thought I saw a strange-looking man outside the house. Did you _____ him?
(c) I was in such a hurry that I didn't _____ what the weather was like.
(d) I have often heard tourists _____ favourably on the number of parks in the city.

17 **souvenir** (something bought or taken home as a reminder of a visit, occasion etc.)
     memory (something remembered, ability to remember)
(a) I bought a model policeman as a _____ of my visit to London.
(b) Playing football with friends is perhaps my happiest childhood _____ .
(c) I still have an old Spanish railway timetable that I kept as a _____ .
(d) My _____ isn't so good as I get old.

18 **stamp** (postage-stamp, official mark on document etc.)
     print (picture made from engraved block)
(a) What value _____ do I need for this letter, please?
(b) Most of his work was oil paintings and water-colours but he also produced the occasional _____ .
(c) I bought a beautiful _____ by Hokusai, the Japanese artist.
(d) At the border, the official put a _____ in my passport showing the date and place.

19 **reunion** (gathering of old friends, colleagues after separation)
     meeting (gathering of people for social or formal discussion)
(a) We have a _____ at the office every Friday to talk about plans and problems.
(b) I haven't seen my old school friends for 15 years. It's time someone organised a _____ .
(c) They're having a _____ to discuss plans for a big _____ of soldiers who fought in the Battle of Alamein.

20 **sympathetic** (showing sympathy or understanding, willing to listen to others' problems)
     nice (pleasant)
(a) She was a very _____ little girl. Everyone liked her.
(b) He's usually rather impatient and unfriendly, but I must say he was very _____ when I told him about my family problems.
(c) It was a _____ party. I enjoyed it.
(d) The police were very _____ to my complaint about the noise but said they could do nothing about it.

21 **corps** [kɔː] (special military of diplomatic etc. group of people)
     corpse [kɔːps] (dead body)
(a) The _____ was examined by a pathologist to determine the cause of death.
(b) Members of the Diplomatic _____ have a special legal status when they are abroad.
(c) There is to be a reorganisation of the Royal Army Medical _____ .
(d) When the king died, his _____ was wrapped in gold robes and laid in a stone coffin.

22 **voyage** (journey by sea)
     journey (travelling from one place to another)
(a) The liner *Titanic* struck an iceberg and sank on her very first _____ .
(b) My _____ to work every morning takes about 40 minutes.
(c) He went on a long _____ across Asia.
(d) Before the opening of the Suez Canal, the _____ from Europe to India round Africa took several weeks.

23 **legend** (very old, possibly untrue, story)
    key (set of symbols and their meanings on a map etc.)
(a) The _____ of King Witold and his gold palace is a very amusing story but it has no foundation in fact.
(b) The _____ at the bottom of the map explains the various symbols used.
(c) The different parts of the diagram are numbered and you'll find the _____ to these on the opposite page.
(d) Some people regard the account as historical fact while others dismiss it as a _____ .

24 **become** (grow, develop into)
    obtain (get possession of)
(a) Visitors to Australia from certain countries must _____ a visa.
(b) His only ambition was to _____ rich.
(c) As the electric current passes through it, it will _____ hot.
(d) You can _____ the necessary information from any post office.

25 **on the contrary** (introduces contradiction, opposite)
    on the other hand (introduces counter-argument)
(a) Good Lord, I'm not rich! _____ , I'm constantly in debt.
(b) She's very intelligent, but _____ she's apt to be impatient.
(c) Yes, it's a very cosmopolitan city. _____ , it's very expensive.
(d) I don't think he'll pass the exam. _____ , I think he'll almost certainly fail.

26 **critic** (reviewer, person who writes newspaper article on new book, film etc.)
    review (article written by critic)
(a) Have you read the *Daily Express* _____ of that new Spanish film?
(b) She was the book-_____ of a literary magazine.
(c) One _____ wrote a very bad _____ of my play. The others liked it.

CLICHÉS

A cliché is an expression that has been used over and over again. Many people scorn clichés as unoriginal, hackneyed terms to be avoided, but in fact they have become clichés because they are so apt and fit the situation so well. Anything can become a cliché if it is overused. Here is a selection.

Crime doesn't pay.	**Life is what you make it.**
Time flies.	**Isn't nature wonderful!**
Home sweet home.	**Her death was a merciful release.**
It's a funny old world.	**He is a pillar of the community.**

Idiom

Alliterative Expressions

1 'Alliteration' is the repeated use of the same letter or sound, usually the first letter of successive words. It is often used in poetic language ('borne on the swollen, swaying, swishing seas'), publicity ('Buy Brown's Best British Biscuits') and newspaper headlines ('Fighting Football Fans Face Fines'). It is also found in the following common colloquial expressions. Put each one in its correct place in the sentences below.

ship-shape   **rat race**   **wishy-washy**
mish-mash   **chit-chat**   **brickbats**

(a) Tired of the ceaseless pressure of the competitive business world, he decided to leave the _____ and take over a small newsagent's shop in the country.
(b) A politician must be strong enough to withstand the _____ which are constantly directed at him by the media.
(c) He's a serious, rather cold man. He likes to get to the point straightaway in conversation and not waste time in idle _____ .
(d) I like to see everything neat and tidy, everything in its place. I like to keep everything _____ .
(e) Michael Wilson's latest play is a confusing mixture. It is neither a comedy, a serious work nor a musical, but a _____ of all three.
(f) A company's annual report must be clearly written and contain only the necessary facts. A report which is vague and _____ is useless and makes a bad impression.

2   Instructions as above.

zigzag   **sing-song**   **pitter-patter**
flip-flops   **sob-story**   **creepy-crawly**

(a) I heard the _____ of rain on the window panes.
(b) It's too steep to climb straight up the side of the hill. Most people _____ to make it easier.
(c) He tried to get money from me by telling a _____ about losing his job and being ill, but I didn't believe him.
(d) If little Louise sees a beetle or a spider, she screams, 'There's a _____ !'.
(e) To keep our spirits up on the long journey we had a _____ .
(f) _____ are cheap, open sandals, each consisting of a rubber sole and a strap between the toes.

'GHOTI'

The writer George Bernard Shaw thought English spelling was ridiculous. He demonstrated this by saying that the word 'fish' could be spelt 'ghoti', the -'gh' pronounced as in 'enough', the '-o' as in 'women' and the '-ti' as in 'station'.

3   Instructions as above.

tittle-tattle　　　　**hot-head**　　　　**riff-raff**
weight-watcher　　　**tell-tale**　　　　**topsy-turvy**

(a)   He wants to be slimmer, so he's become a _____ . He's on a strict diet.
(b)   He's a very calm, moderate person, but his brother is a _____ who is liable to get very upset and even violent over political matters.
(c)   Oh, I don't believe those stories they tell about him. They're just _____ .
(d)   'The club I belong to is very exclusive,' he said snobbishly, 'They only accept upper-class people, not ordinary, vulgar _____.'
(e)   He denied any involvement in the murder, but police found _____ traces of blood on his clothing.
(f)   In the morning he found the whole office _____ and realised it had been burgled.

Animals

1   Put each of the following phrases in its correct place in the sentences.

dog's life　　　　**dog-collar**　　　　**wolf in sheep's clothing**
bookworm　　　　**wolf-whistles**　　　**wild-goose chase**
underdog　　　　　**puppy fat**　　　　 **stag party**

(a)   He's always reading. He'll read anything. He's a real _____.
(b)   He's a very informal priest. He rarely wears a _____.
(c)   Little Johnnie's parents were worried that he was very big, but the doctor told them not to worry as it was only _____.
(d)   He was elected President as a man of peace and moderation, but when he began a reign of terror, people realised he was a_____.
(e)   Some girls appreciate _____ but others are embarrassed by them.
(f)   It's hard work – not much money, no time to enjoy yourself. It's a _____.
(g)   'Sorry I can't invite you, Mary,' said Peter, 'but it's a _____.'
(h)   Most people want the weaker side to win for a change. It's human nature to support the _____.
(i)   I went all over the place trying to get what I wanted but I had no success at all. It was a _____.

2   Instructions as above.

fly on the wall　　　**dog-eared**　　　　**frog in my throat**
guinea pig　　　　　**pigeon-holes**　　　**bird's-eye-view**
cat's eyes

(a)   After a book has been used a lot, it tends to get a bit _____.
(b)   I'd love to be a _____ when the American and Russian leaders meet for a private talk.
(c)   From that mountain you'll get a _____ of the town and lake.
(d)   Down the middle of the road, reflecting the cars' headlights, are the _____.
(e)   I was once a _____ in a medical experiment to test a new drug.
(f)   Can I have a glass of water? I've got a _____.
(g)   In offices and hotels, letters are often placed in little, open-ended compartments called _____ labelled with the letters of the alphabet.

3   Use each of the following animals as a verb by putting it in a suitable form in its correct space in the sentences below.

fox   monkey   worm   hound
dog   ram   duck   badger

(a) The thief in the stolen car refused to stop so the police were forced to _____ it with their own car.
(b) This machine is complicated and dangerous so don't _____ about with it.
(c) The children _____ their father to buy them a dog until he finally gave in and did so.
(d) He complained that because of his political beliefs he had been _____ by the press.
(e) To avoid being seen he _____ down behind the hedge.
(f) He tried to avoid telling me but after half an hour I managed to _____ the truth out of him.
(g) He managed to _____ his pursuers by changing cars three times and then escaping in disguise.
(h) All through her life she was _____ by misfortune.

Body

1   Parts of the body appear in some colloquial idiomatic adjectives describing various human states and characteristics, e.g. 'heavy-hearted' means 'sad'. For each adjective on the left below find the word or phrase on the right which has the same meaning.

(a) stout-hearted   generous
(b) tight-fisted   brave, resolute
(c) open-handed   with very good hearing
(d) hard-headed   conceited, self-important
(e) big-headed   hypocritical
(f) weak-kneed   silent, unwilling to speak
(g) sharp-eared   mean, not generous
(h) tight-lipped   insensitive to criticism
(i) two-faced   businesslike, unemotional
(j) starry-eyed   cowardly, nervous
(k) thick-skinned   over-romantic

NATIONALITY IDIOMS

English often uses the names of other countries in common phrases. If two or more people at a restaurant or pub **go dutch**, they all pay for themselves. If you can't make sense of written instructions, you say **'It's all Greek to me'**. If warm, dry weather continues into autumn, it's **an Indian summer**. Do you know what **Dutch courage** is? And where would you see a **Mexican wave**? And what is **Russian roulette**?

2   The following parts of the body are used as verbs in the sentences below. Put each one in its correct place.

shin	head	mouth	finger	back
thumb	head	foot	shoulder	elbow

(a)   I think we'd better _____ for the station. Our train leaves in half an hour.
(b)   It's your fault! Don't leave me to _____ all the blame!
(c)   There was a crowd of people there. I had to _____ my way through.
(d)   They decided to _____ their way round Europe. They're experienced hitch-hikers.
(e)   If customers _____ a book a lot, it gets dirty.
(f)   I'm having my house painted. It's very expensive. I don't know how I'm going to _____ the bill.
(g)   Bob couldn't hear me because of the noise so I had to _____ what I wanted to say.
(h)   He's very fit and strong. Watch him _____ up that tree like a monkey.
(i)   It has been announced that the Foreign Minister will _____ a delegation to visit China next month.
(j)   A large manufacturing firm has offered to _____ the Himalayan Expedition.

Collocations

Certain common adjectives are sometimes emphasised, especially in colloquial language, with the addition of another adjective or noun in front of them, e.g. 'The water was icy cold.' 'The road was dead straight'. 'Icy' and 'dead' in these sentences mean 'extremely' or 'absolutely'.

1   Put each word from the following list in its correct space in the sentences.

wide	dog	pitch	brand
stone	dirt	stark	bone

(a)   I wouldn't employ him. He's _____ idle.
(b)   It's an amazing price, _____ cheap!
(c)   I was _____ tired after such a hard day's work.
(d)   He couldn't hear a thing. He was _____ deaf.
(e)   It's not second-hand. It's _____ new.
(f)   This room's freezing and the window's _____ open!
(g)   Here's a photo of him at three months, _____ naked.
(h)   It was _____ dark. I couldn't see a thing.

2   Instructions as above.

fast	bone	razor	blind
wide	crystal	paper	flat

(a)   She had a _____ sharp mind.
(b)   She went to bed at seven and she was _____ asleep by ten past.
(c)   The sea near those rocks is _____ clear.
(d)   There's been no rain for months and the land is _____ dry.
(e)   Sorry, I can't lend you anything. I'm _____ broke.
(f)   He was _____ drunk. He couldn't even walk properly.
(g)   The neighbours hear everything we say. The walls are _____ thin.
(h)   It was 2 a.m. but I was still _____ awake.

3   Certain nouns are often preceded, in the same way as the adjectives above, by adjectives (or sometimes by nouns used as adjectives) to emphasise their completeness and convey the meaning of 'extreme' or 'total'. Put each word from the following list in its correct place in the sentences below.

thin   **all-out**   **dire**   **blank**
blind   **bitter**   **rock**   **broad**

(a) We'll never give up the struggle. We'll fight to the _____ end.
(b) He was never seen again. He just seemed to disappear into _____ air.
(c) Those starving people are in _____ need of food.
(d) I had last heard of her in Australia 20 years before. When she walked in, I looked at her in _____ amazement.
(e) Crime is very prevalent there. People are robbed in the street in _____ daylight.
(f) The fighting is escalating rapidly. Soon it will be _____ war.
(g) Prices have been falling rapidly. When they reach _____-bottom, I'll buy.
(h) His followers' attitude to him was nothing short of _____ devotion.

Colour

1   Put each of the following phrases in its correct place in the sentences below.

out of the blue   **in the red**   **a black sheep**
once in a blue moon   **red tape**   **green with envy**
to have green fingers   **in black and white**   **to catch someone red-handed**

(a) The offer of a job sounded very good on the phone but I shan't believe it till I have it _____.
(b) I must remind you that this is a non-smoking office. I suspect that some of you have been smoking. If I happen _____, I'm afraid it will mean dismissal.
(c) To import firearms into Britain you'll have to fill in a lot of forms. There's a lot of _____.
(d) If you want to be a successful gardener, of course you've got _____.
(e) The rest of the family were respectable, honest people but he was always in trouble. I'm afraid he was _____.
(f) When I saw him in a new sports car, I was _____.
(g) Tourists often go to the Louvre but most Parisians only go _____.
(h) The firm is _____. It owes a lot of money.
(i) I had lost touch with Jack, and then one night he arrived at my flat right _____. What a surprise!

2   Instructions as above.

red-carpet treatment   **to see red**   **rose-coloured spectacles**
a red herring   **a white-collar job**   **a green belt**
blue-eyed boy   **a white lie**

(a) Naturally the President's wife received _____ on her visit.
(b) He said he didn't want to have _____ and sit in an office all day.
(c) All round the city there is _____ of open country where building is restricted.
(d) She loves animals and tends _____ when she sees one being badly treated.

(e) He told _____ to avoid hurting his wife's feelings.

(f) Everyone thinks he'll be Director of the firm one day. He's the _____.

(g) Be realistic. You can't go through life looking at the world through _____.

(h) In class pupils sometimes introduce _____ to distract the teacher from his subject.

Fictional Characters in Everyday Language

1   The following are names of characters in popular fiction. They are so well-known (even by those who have never read or even heard of the original work) that they are often used in ordinary conversation. Put each one in its correct place in the sentences below.

Robin Hood	**Man Friday**	**James Bond**	**Robinson Crusoe**
Superman	**Peter Pan**	**Billy Bunter**	**Scrooge**

(a) During the war he was sent on dangerous secret missions abroad. Very exciting! He was a sort of _____.

(b) I think Alan should go on a diet and get more exercise. He's beginning to look like _____.

(c) He still has very youthful enthusiasms, and he's as slim and fit as he was 20 years ago. He's a _____.

(d) There are times when most of us would like to escape from all the pressures of city life and live a more simple, basic kind of _____ existence.

(e) Come on! I've never met anyone so reluctant to spend money, you _____!

(f) He's not very practical. What he needs is someone to look after him and do everything for him. He needs a _____.

(g) The firm is doing very badly and facing bankruptcy. I don't think it can survive. We don't just want a new director. We want a _____.

(h) Well, yes, he was a criminal and he stole a lot of money, but he helped a lot of people with it. He was a bit of a _____.

2   Instructions as above.

Walter Mitty	**Jekyll and Hyde**	**Little Lord Fauntleroy**	**Tarzan**
Big Brother	**Rip Van Winkle**	**Sherlock Holmes**	**Cinderella**

(a) He's a strange person. Usually he's very pleasant and reasonable, but there are times when he gets very bad-tempered and almost violent. He's got a _____ personality.

(b) How on earth did you guess his nationality, occupation and all those other things about him just from his appearance? You're a proper _____.

(c) I don't like this new government proposal to put details of everyone's private life on computers. I can see it will mean greater efficiency and all that, but, well, it's a bit like _____, isn't it?

(d) I think the neighbours' kids should be allowed a bit of freedom to wear what they like and get dirty having fun, not made to look like _____.

(e) She's really exploited by her family. They make her do everything for them, cook, clean … She's a sort of _____.

(f) He's a body-builder and weight-lifter. Have you seen him in a swimsuit? He looks like _____.

(g) He sounds very impressive when he talks about his adventures and achievements, but it's all fantasy. He's a _____ character.

(h) Come on, _____, wake up! It's nearly lunch-time.

Food

1   Put each of the following colloquial words or phrases in its correct place in the sentences below.

the salt of the earth	**cup of tea**	**peanuts**	**no picnic**
a butter-fingers	**a vegetable**	**the cream**	**nuts**
a piece of cake	**full of beans**	**in a jam**	**sour grapes**

(a)   Throw it to me! Oh, I've dropped it! I am _____.
(b)   I said I'd pay him today, but my money's in the bank and it's just closed. Now I'm _____.
(c)   You'll have to offer her a high salary for an easy job. An experienced editor like her wouldn't do the job for _____.
(d)   He never wants to do anything interesting. He just sits around all day. He's a bit of _____.
(e)   It'll be cold and wet in the mountains. And we'll have heavy rucksacks to carry. It'll be _____.
(f)   That firm only employs the very best graduates. They only take _____.
(g)   I think people who help the old, sick and homeless are _____.
(h)   He's a bit tired and lifeless now, but after a nap he'll be _____.
(i)   She now says she didn't really want the job that she failed to get, but I think it's just _____.
(j)   That's a crazy idea of hers. She must be _____.
(k)   She likes literature and classical music. Discothèques are not her _____.
(l)   The exam was very easy. It was _____.

2   Complete the colloquial similies below with the correct items from the following list.

hot potato	**cucumber**	**hot cakes**
two peas in a pod	**water**	**beetroot**
toast	**sardines**	**pancake**

(a)   He never panics in a difficult situation. He stays as cool as a _____.
(b)   She was very embarrassed. She went as red as a _____.
(c)   No, we aren't cold. Your flat's very warm. We're as warm as _____.
(d)   There are no hills or slopes for miles around. It's as flat as a _____.
(e)   They're identical twins, as like as _____.
(f)   As soon as his future employers heard he had a criminal record, they dropped him like a _____.
(g)   That singer's new record is in great demand. It's selling like _____.
(h)   In the rush-hour buses, people are packed like _____.
(i)   She's very extravagant. She spends money like _____.

LETTER-WORDS

The first part of each of the following words consists of a single letter. What do the words mean?

A-bomb	**T-shirt**	**U-turn**
E-mail	**V-neck**	**T-junction**
V-formation	**X-ray**	**A-line**

'Hand'

1   Put each of the following phrases in its correct place in the sentences below.

cap in hand   **to hand**   **offhand**
out of hand   **hand-to-mouth**   **underhand**

(a) I'm afraid I don't know her address _____. I'll tell you tomorrow after I've looked it up.
(b) He wouldn't have minded so much if they had told him to his face that they wanted to dismiss him. It was the _____ way in which they did it that upset him.
(c) I'd rather borrow from the bank at high interest than go _____ to my father.
(d) The situation is now _____. The authorities admit that they cannot control the rioting and crime.
(e) He makes just enough money to provide for his basic daily needs. It's a wretched, _____ existence.
(f) She always has pencil and paper _____ in case she suddenly sees an interesting person or place she wants to sketch.

2   Instructions as above.

high handed   **short-handed**   **in good hands**
offhand   **empty-handed**   **single-handed**

(a) His manner was deceptively casual and _____. In fact he was a very serious, decisive person.
(b) We left the car with my brother-in-law. He's very careful and reliable so we knew it was _____.
(c) The shops were shut so I couldn't buy her a present. I felt bad arriving _____.
(d) I think you were rather _____ in dismissing him without consulting me or giving him a chance to explain.
(e) Three people were off sick at the office today so we were very _____.
(f) She was the first woman to sail the Atlantic _____. Her only problem was loneliness.

3   Instructions as above.

to wash his hands of   **to have a hand in**   **to give him a free hand**
to have the upper hand   **to keep his hand in**   **to win hands down**

(a) I think we ought _____ and let him carry out the scheme as he thinks best without any interference from us.
(b) He gave up playing the piano professionally years ago but he still likes _____ by playing a little from time to time.
(c) He wants nothing more to do with the idea. He just wants _____ the whole thing.
(d) The guerrillas are reported _____. The government forces are very much on the defensive.
(e) My older brother always beat me easily at tennis. He always used _____.
(f) He is thought _____ a gold-smuggling operation now going on but the police can't prove it.

Names

1 Some common names appear in idiomatic expressions. Put each of the following items in its correct place in the sentences below.

peeping Tom   **smart Alec**   **Jack of all trades**
doubting Thomas   **bobby**   **Tom, Dick or Harry**

(a) A British policeman is sometimes called a '_____'. The name comes from Sir Robert Peel, the founder of the first London police force.
(b) It is often said of someone who can do many different things that he is a _____.
(c) Someone who spies on other people, especially by looking through their windows, is called a _____.
(d) Oh, don't take any notice of him. He thinks he knows everything. He's just a _____.
(e) He's a real snob. He's only interested in people who are rich or famous. He won't talk to any _____.
(f) When the Wright brothers invented the first aeroplane which actually flew, there was many a _____ who said that air-travel would never be commercially successful.

2 Instructions as above.

keeping up with the Joneses   **robbing Peter to pay Paul**
I don't know him from Adam   **before you could say Jack Robinson**

(a) No, I'm sure I've never met him. He's a complete stranger. Really, _____.
(b) The couple next door are very conscious of their social position. They've got a new car, a modern kitchen, trendy new clothes. They don't really need them. They're just _____.
(c) It's ridiculous to borrow from your uncle to settle your debt to your cousin. That's just _____.
(d) One man insulted another and suddenly, _____, they were involved in a violent fight.

LITERARY OR POETIC WORDS

A certain class of words is mainly found in old-fashioned English or poetry. However, it is worth paying attention to them because they are still used in jokes and ironic language. You might hear, 'You've been imbibing' (drinking) or 'He's my deadly foe' (enemy). Here is a short list.

toil (work)	tidings (news)	betwixt (between)
behold (see)	fare (food)	penurious (poor)
swift (fast)	peruse (read)	slumber (sleep)
demise (death)	scribe (writer)	thoroughfare (street)
attire (clothes)	hale (healthy)	converse (talk)

Numbers

1 Put each of the following expressions in its correct place in the sentences below.

one-armed bandit   **catch 22 situation**   **one-track mind**
two-edged compliment   **one-man band**   **four-letter word**

(a) She said I looked very good for my age. That was rather a _____, wasn't it?
(b) A gambling machine where you put a coin in and pull a lever at the side is sometimes called a _____.
(c) The only thing he thinks about is money. He's got a _____.
(d) Television viewers protested at the use of a _____ in a programme last night. They said they were disgusted and shocked.
(e) Although he has occasional help, the firm is really a _____.
(f) You can't get a job without experience and you can't get experience without a job. It's a _____.

2 Instructions as above.

to have second thoughts   **on first name terms**   **third-rate**
in her seventh heaven   **the third degree**   **sixth sense**
at the eleventh hour   **to play second fiddle**

(a) The security forces denied accusations that they had used _____ on prisoners to make them confess.
(b) He was a brilliant journalist who seemed to have a _____ which told him when and where something important was going to happen.
(c) It's a very friendly company to work in. Everyone's _____.
(d) She was _____ when she actually met her favourite film-star. She'll never forget it.
(e) He likes to be his own boss. He'll never agree _____ to anyone else.
(f) No, it wasn't a very good film. In fact it was pretty _____.
(g) At first she liked him, but now she's beginning _____.
(h) Our financial problems were so great that we thought we'd have to sell our house, but _____ my father-in-law lent us some money.

AMERICAN ENGLISH 2

There are a few small differences in the use of prepositions and adverbs between British and American English. How would a British person say the following American sentences?

Washington is very different **than** New York.
The exhibition continues **through** 30 April.
He's shy **around** girls.
There was a large field **in the back of** the house.
I haven't seen Joe **in** years.
This work isn't good enough. Do it **over**.
I was there from a quarter **of** nine to a quarter **after** ten.
Mary Perez made a speech **in** behalf of the whole class.
The school is named **for** its founder.

Pairs

1   Put each of the following colloquial 'pair-phrases' in its correct place in the sentences below.

cloak and dagger   **length and breadth**   **hard and fast**
chop and change   **song and dance**   **by and large**
pins and needles   **tooth and nail**   **prim and proper**
touch and go

(a) It was _____ whether the police would get to the scene of the accident in time.
(b) She's very strict in moral matters and rather a snob. She's very _____.
(c) I agree that the shop treated you very badly. But just write a polite letter of complaint. It's not worth making a _____ about it.
(d) Of course a few pupils were lazy, but _____ the children were interested and hard-working.
(e) If you take a decision, you must stick to it. You can't _____ all the time.
(f) When the old man died, his greedy relatives fought _____ over his will.
(g) We don't regard our entry requirements as _____ rules. We are prepared to be flexible.
(h) He knows Brazil very well. He's travelled the _____ of the country.
(i) I like exciting novels about spies and conspiracies. I love that _____ stuff.
(j) If you've been sitting in one position for a long time without moving, you sometimes get _____.

2   Instructions as above.

safe and sound   **ups and downs**   **odds and ends**   **up and about**
sick and tired   **to and fro**   **ins and outs**   **down and out**
pros and cons   **spick and span**

(a) I'm _____ of his continual bad behaviour.
(b) She's very house-proud. Her kitchen is always _____.
(c) I just keep various _____ in that drawer, nothing special.
(d) Like everyone else, she has her _____ of course, but on the whole she's quite satisfied with life.
(e) He lost everything, family, job, money, home … Now he's _____ and sleeping in the park.
(f) You should consider the _____ carefully before you make a decision.
(g) She's ill in bed, but she'll be _____ in a couple of days.
(h) The parents were beginning to worry but finally the children arrived home _____.
(i) This ferry-boat operates between England and France. It just goes _____ all the time.
(j) He's the right man for the job. He's experienced. He knows the _____ of the business.

Phrasal Verbs

1   Put each of the following phrasal verbs in its correct place in the sentences below.

get down	**bring up**	**take down**	**call off**
try out	**bring up**	**put up**	**see off**

(a)   Don't worry about the journey to the airport. I'm coming to _____ you _____.

(b)   The other car didn't stop after the accident but luckily I was able to _____ its number.

(c)   The car's in quite good condition but you can _____ it _____ before you make any decision to buy.

(d)   Would you like to _____ any other matters before the meeting closes?

(e)   Stop worrying about it. Don't let this failure _____ you _____.

(f)   I'm afraid we'll have to _____ the meeting _____. Alice and John can't come.

(g)   Her parents died when she was eight and her uncle decided to _____ her _____ himself.

(h)   I've got a spare room, so I can _____ you _____ if you're ever here again.

2   Instructions as above.

run down	**bear out**	**make up**	**let down**
rule out	**put forward**	**put off**	**leave out**

(a)   I'm depending on you to pay me back the money on Monday. Please don't _____ me _____.

(b)   To cover his absence he decided to _____ a completely false story about being involved in a car accident.

(c)   If you think I'm wrong, check in the encyclopaedia. I'm sure it will _____ me _____.

(d)   Because of pressure of work, he had to _____ his summer holiday until October.

(e)   We want to give younger players a chance in the team. That's why we've decided to _____ you _____ of next Saturday's match.

(f)   They're very two-faced. They're very nice to her when she's there, but they _____ her _____ behind her back.

(g)   I'd like to _____ a proposal. I suggest we start production in May.

(h)   The government intend to take very serious measures against this interference in their country's affairs. They do not _____ the possibility of military action.

3   Instructions as above.

give away	**do up**	**turn away**	**put up**
look up	**put off**	**pull down**	**turn out**

(a)   The authorities intend to _____ these old buildings and _____ a modern office block in their place.

(b)   They'll never believe you're American. Your accent will _____ you _____ immediately.

(c)   If you persist in refusing to pay the rent for this flat, we shall have no option but to _____ you _____.

(d)   When I was in New York, I was able to _____ several old friends I hadn't seen for years.

(e) We're very sorry to have to _____ you _____, but I'm afraid the hotel is fully booked.

(f) The flat hasn't been very well looked after, but I think that after I _____ it _____ it'll look very nice.

(g) The old-fashioned appearance of the hotel might _____ some people, but in fact it's really very modern and comfortable inside.

4   Instructions as above.

take to	**stand for**	**get over**	**account for**
come into	**get round**	**run into**	**take after**

(a) The initials V.I.P. _____ Very Important Person.

(b) Scientists are mystified by the sudden increase in the world's temperature. They are quite unable to _____ it.

(c) I don't think he'll ever completely _____ his wife's death. He'll always miss her.

(d) John works in that office. I quite often _____ him in the streets round here.

(e) I can't think of a way to _____ the problem.

(f) She has a very pleasant manner. I'm sure the children will _____ her at once.

(g) He expects to _____ a lot of money in his grandfather's will.

(h) My father and I have the same character. I _____ him much more than my mother.

5   Instructions as above.

make up for	**be up to**	**look down on**	**catch up with**
put up with	**be up to**	**do away with**	**go back on**

(a) If they _____ their promise, I'll never trust them again.

(b) You must make your suggestion to the director. Then it'll _____ him to decide.

(c) He missed a month's school through illness, so now he'll have to work hard to _____ the other pupils.

(d) I don't think I can _____ this noise any longer. I'm going mad.

(e) I'm sorry we had to cancel the party, but to _____ it let's all go to the cinema.

(f) The growing use of credit cards may ultimately _____ the use of cash altogether.

(g) There are some strange noises coming from Jane's room. What on earth can she _____?

(h) I'm afraid they're very snobbish. They _____ their poorer relations.

6   Instructions as above.

break up	**go off**	**come out**	**break out**
turn in	**look up**	**turn up**	**fall through**

(a) It's past midnight and I'm tired. I think I'll _____.

(b) I waited nearly an hour for them, but they didn't _____.

(c) After all the trouble you've taken, I hope your plans don't _____.

(d) There is a very real fear that war may _____ soon.

(e) We've had some hard times recently, but I think things are beginning to _____.

(f) The emergency services thought that the bomb might _____ at any moment.

(g) The schools _____ next week. It's almost holiday-time.

(h) Her new book is due to _____ next month. I wonder what the critics will think of it.

7   Instructions as above.

go down	**drop off**	**break down**	**come up**
fall out	**drop in**	**fall off**	**hold on**

(a)   The number of tourists visiting Spain is at its peak in July and August and begins to _____ in September.

(b)   The subject of higher salaries will probably _____ at the meeting.

(c)   Don't get so nervous about your speech tonight. I'm sure it'll _____ very well.

(d)   She's not a very strong person. I'm afraid she might _____ when she hears the news.

(e)   They haven't spoken to each other since that argument about the taxi fare. How silly to _____ over such a trivial thing.

(f)   I think we're going in the wrong direction. _____, I'll look at the map.

(g)   I live at 32, Rutherford Street. _____ if you're in the district.

(h)   The meeting was long and the room was hot. I was afraid I might _____.

Rhyming Expressions

1   A number of common colloquial expressions consist of rhyming parts. Put each of the following expressions in its correct place in the sentences below.

big-wigs	**pell-mell**	**higgledy-piggledy**	**brain-drain**
nitty-gritty	**prime-time**	**humdrum**	**culture-vulture**

(a)   We've got some important visitors coming to see the factory tomorrow. They're government inspectors, Members of Parliament, officials from the Ministry and other _____.

(b)   The programme is only of limited interest. I can't understand why it's shown on _____ television.

(c)   The two world leaders met and after the usual greetings and formalities got down to the _____ of their talks.

(d)   He goes to all the new plays, reads the new novels, loves art and ballet. He's a real _____.

(e)   After the robbery everything was in a mess, _____, all over the place.

(f)   She'd like to find a more interesting, exciting job. She finds her present work very _____.

(g)   It's been a terrible morning. I overslept, rushed out _____ to the bus-stop, missed the bus, had to get a taxi …

(h)   The _____ of doctors, scientists and academics leaving this country is having a serious effect on our health service, industries and universities.

2   Instructions as above.

silly-billy	**hanky-panky**	**space-race**	**walkie-talkie**
mumbo-jumbo	**willy-nilly**	**fun-run**	**roly-poly**

(a)   A policeman usually carries a _____ so that he can keep in touch with his police station.

(b)   5,000 people are taking part in a five-mile _____ on Sunday to raise money for charity.

(c)   You've put on weight. You're getting quite _____.

(d) Oh, I am a _____. I've bought salt and I meant to buy sugar.

(e) The competition between the United States and the Soviet Union in the field of rockets and inter-planetary exploration is often called the _____.

(f) She did not believe in having a religious wedding and considered the church service to be just a lot of _____.

(g) In the army you don't have much choice where to go. You're sent where you're needed, _____.

(h) There have been accusations of illegalities, suspicious irregularities and other _____ during the elections. There's going to be an inquiry.

3   Instructions above.

wine and dine   **moan and groan**   **meals-on-wheels**
wear and tear   **la-di-da**   **make or break**

(a) Old people who cannot cook for themselves easily are entitled to use the _____ service.

(b) This is Wayne Smith's last chance to show if he is good enough for the football team. It's _____ day for him.

(c) She was very affected in her accent and manner. Most people thought she was very _____.

(d) After twelve years it's only natural that your furniture is showing signs of _____.

(e) Come to the best restaurant in town, where you can _____ in style.

(f) If you find so much to complain about in your job, either do something about it or resign. Don't just _____.

Status

Use the correct phrase from the following list to replace each of the phrases in italics in the sentences below.

The headmaster-to be   **The so-called headmaster**
The late headmaster   **The would-be headmaster**
The present headmaster   **The ex-headmaster**
The headmaster present   **The stop-gap headmaster**
The actual headmaster   **The sacked headmaster**
The headmaster in question

(a) The *man determined to be headmaster* made a speech.

(b) The *headmaster, who is now dead,* made a speech.

(c) The *headmaster who was at the occasion* made a speech.

(d) The *man who had previously been headmaster* made a speech.

(e) The *man who is now headmaster* made a speech.

(f) The *headmaster who was dismissed* made a speech.

(g) The *headmaster himself* made a speech.

(h) The *man who was temporarily acting as headmaster until someone was appointed permanently* made a speech.

(i) The *headmaster who is the subject of discussion* made a speech.

(j) The *man who was due to take up his appointment as headmaster* made a speech.

(k) The *headmaster, who I think is very bad at his job*, made a speech.

Time

1 Put each of the following phrases in its correct place in the sentences.

at the time   **for the time being**   **in time**
at one time   **at times**   **on time**

(a) _____ the streets of the city were lit by gas, but that was at least a hundred years ago.
(b) Soon after they met, they decided to get married. _____ it seemed an ideal match. Within a few years, however, their different personalities began to cause friction.
(c) She's quite happy in Portugal on the whole, but of course she misses Brazil _____.
(d) We're painting our son's bedroom, so _____ he's sleeping in our room.
(e) The trains are very punctual. They always leave _____.
(f) When she heard her father was dying, she immediately went to the hospital and arrived just _____.

2 Instructions as above.

pressed for time   **in his time**   **at the same time**
behind the times   **before my time**   **in no time**

(a) My father's been to almost every country in the world _____.
(b) We must keep up to date. We can't compete successfully with other firms if we get _____ in our methods.
(c) He's looking forward to starting his new job, but _____ he's a bit nervous.
(d) I'm afraid I can't talk to you at the moment. I'm a bit _____.
(e) Someone called Wilkins used to be the head of this firm, but I never met him. It was _____.
(f) She's very bright and quick. She learnt to use a computer _____.

3 Instructions as above.

all in good time   **time after time**   **for old time's sake**
in the nick of time   **about time too**   **time on his hands**

(a) The firemen got the children out _____. Less than a minute later the building collapsed.
(b) You can have a bicycle, and I'll get you a camera. But not yet. _____.
(c) I met an old school-friend the other day. He was down on his luck and out of work. I doubt if he's really very efficient but I got him a job in my firm just _____.
(d) Ah, here you are! _____! I've been waiting an hour.
(e) Having been busy all his life, he finds it strange to have _____ now that he's retired. He doesn't know what to do with himself.
(f) I've warned them about it _____ but they never listen.

Identification

Objects

In each of the following passages someone is referring to a well-known object. Identify each object and give at least five words which helped you to decide.

(a) The mudguards are a bit loose and quite a bit of wet comes up at me when it's raining and the gears don't work very well and there are a couple of spokes missing. And maybe I should replace the pedals. They're worn and my feet slipped off this morning and I had to hang onto the handlebars and pull up quickly. Luckily the brake-blocks were OK.

(b) It's quite posh-looking, made of calf, hand-sewn, with brass hinges. There are compartments inside the lid for various documents. It's 16" x 12" x 3" and it's got my initials in gold near the handle.

(c) I can easily find the volume knob to turn it up because it's on the far right at the bottom. And then there's the brightness control next to it and then the buttons for the different channels. The picture's good except for a bit of a flicker sometimes and there's interference when someone's using a vacuum-cleaner. Otherwise it's OK.

(d) The frontispiece is a photograph of Churchill. It's very much thumbed and coffee-stained, the binding is loose and the spine is so faded that you can scarcely read the title. God knows where the dust-jacket went. It was pretty tattered anyway.

(e) It's nothing special, not a grand, just an ordinary old upright. Needs tuning, as you'll hear. Open the lid and you'll see the keyboard. The pedals are a bit stiff. Sit down. Have a go.

(f) The face is a bit scratched and the strap is only plastic, with a cheap metal buckle. You wind it by turning the little knob. The case is stainless steel. It cost me about fifteen quid.

(g) There's not much foliage at the moment. It's deciduous. But it still looks lovely to me. I like the rough bark and the sturdy trunk. Just think, a hundred years ago it was just a sapling. I hope they don't plan to fell it.

(h) Take a look at this. Hold it. Touch the trigger. Spin the chamber. That's where you put the cartridges in. This is the safety-catch, but don't worry, it's not loaded. In fact I've got no ammunition. How would you like to find yourself staring into the muzzle of a thing like this?

(i) Let me unfold it. Here's the scale at the bottom, and the key to the various symbols is in the corner. The relief is shown by contour-lines. I love these things. I should have been a cartographer.

Newspaper Parts

Below are 18 typical extracts from different parts of a newspaper. Identify each one with one of the following words or phrases.

obituary	football report	television preview	headline
gossip column	auction report	travel and holidays	horoscope
new car report	caption	parliamentary report	editorial
gardening tips	recipe		

(a) The word is that Clinton Ross, 32, playboy son of US steel billionaire Dwight Ross, has left his girlfriend, actress Lee-Ann Van Post, 26, and is now in Europe.

(b) Prince Edward (left) enjoys a joke with actor Sam Cool (centre).

(c) PREMIER TO PROBE RIDDLE OF 'SPIES IN MINISTRY'

(d) He received a number of international literary awards, culminating in the Nobel Prize for Literature in 1986. He leaves a widow and two sons.

(e) Today is a good day to do business but a bad one for romance. Don't take members of the opposite sex too seriously today.

(f) Our front page today gives details of the government's new economic proposals. Our readers may think, as we do, that these measures are too little and too late. We say to the government, not for the first time, it is time …

(g) Mix two egg yolks with butter in a frying-pan over a low gas. Add sugar and then …

(h) A pair of silver George II candlesticks fetched £17,000. Bidding was slow for Victorian oil paintings but a landscape by Somers went for £55,000.

(i) Robson equalised with a header from five yards just before the half-time whistle.

(j) The cheapest bucket-shop air-return to Hong Kong is now about £480 and Hong Kong is a good base to visit Macao, China and Taiwan. The best season is …

(k) Mr Richard Caulder (West Hull, Labour) asked if the Minister of Transport could inform MPs of train-fare concessions for pensioners. However, the Speaker declared that …

(l) Now is the time to plant roses. Put trees in at least 2' apart, and cover roots with 6" of soil.

(m) A hard-hitting documentary series starts tonight at 10 p.m. Viewers might be shocked at scenes of …

(n) Road holding and fuel consumption are good but otherwise the performance lacks zip.

The Arts

The following are parts of newspaper reviews of visual and performing arts and literature. Identify the subject of each (film, novel etc.) and give at least six words which helped you to decide.

(a) The first movement is dominated by the strings with only occasional percussion participation. So many bows dancing in unison made this a visual as well as an aural delight and I abandoned my score to watch. In the second movement the wind section takes command, and with such vigour that the baton seems to struggle to keep up rather than the reverse. For once I did not envy the man on the rostrum, and was content with my seat in the stalls.

(b) His favourite medium is now oil, and the canvas which dominates this show, a still-life of bottles, is a masterpiece of representational skill (his early abstracts and collages were never good). His technique is superb. The brush-strokes are invisible, the bottles real. Every section of his palette is used. I shall never again think of bottles as colourless. Every hue of the spectrum is there.

(c) Her weaknesses are characterisation and dialogue. Her strengths are plot and feeling for place. Her characters are two-dimensional, their words wooden, but the events are plausible and the places vividly depicted. The setting is now Mexico City, now Tokyo, now Johannesburg. The twist at the end defies prediction. For once the blurb on the back is true. It says, 'Unputdownable'.

(d) This new young choreographer has given us an exciting and unconventional piece. Called simply *Mixture,* it is indeed influenced by classical, folk, progressive and even tap and ballroom besides. The men are agile and athletic, the girls loose-limbed and supple. The leaps are high, the pirouettes prolonged. What more can you want? The night I went they received a standing ovation.

(e) First-night nerves are notorious, but I have never heard so many lines fluffed, so many cues missed. The prompter was busy last night and the director (and doubtless the backers) in tears. I do not expect this piece to have a long run, but critical reception and box-offices success are often two very different things and, if it does survive, it will have been saved by a number of well-played supporting roles and a stunning set. But the final final curtain cannot, I think, be far off.

Occupations

In each of the following passages someone is talking about his or her occupation. Identify each occupation and give at least five words or phrases which helped you to decide.

(a) Most of my customers are very particular. They want wide lapels or narrow lapels, a single vent or a double vent or no vent at all, turn-ups or plain bottoms. Flared trousers are out nowadays, so are tapered. Everyone wants them straight. Some people are even fussy about the lining. Everyone wants to be trendy.

(b) When I start at 8.30, the baskets are already stacked, the trolleys are lined up near the door and the shelf-fillers have done their work. I make sure I've got a supply of carrier bags and enough change in the till and I'm ready to start.

(c) We get the latest weather briefing from the meteorologists and then we board. We say hello to the cabin crew, do a complete cockpit check, then wait for instructions through the headphones to start taxi-ing out to the runway.

(d) Two discharges today, but five admissions and Mrs Crowther's got to go to theatre this afternoon. They have their mid-morning tea at eleven, then, since it's Tuesday, the specialist will be doing his round at half-past. And there are always relatives' phone-calls to deal with. Next week I'm on night-shift. Excuse me, I must go and change some dressings.

(e) I picked up a fare at the station today. I was in the rank. Smartly-dressed chap. Wanted St Michael's Church. 'Going to a wedding?' I said. 'Yes, and I'm late. Step on it,' he said. I did my best and as I dropped him off I said, 'Doesn't look as if they've started yet.' 'They can't,' he said, 'I'm the bridegroom.' And he didn't give me a tip!

(f) We're fully-dressed in our helmets and protective clothing by the time we arrive. Then we start unrolling the hoses and getting the ladders ready in case they're needed. The worst things are hoax alarms. You can never be sure till you get there whether a call is genuine or not. Some people think it's fun to dial 999 …

(g) I flashed my torch at where they were supposed to go, but they went further down the aisle and along the wrong row. Luckily it was only during the credits or trailer or something, so they didn't disturb people too much. It's usually a pretty routine job, but last week the projectionist fell asleep just before he was supposed to change reels!

Occasions

Each of the following passages is part of a description of an occasion or event. Identify the subject of each description, giving at least six words which helped you to decide.

(a) A warning was given by an anonymous caller saying he represented a separatist movement. The area was evacuated and cordoned off, and attempts were made to defuse the device, but it detonated soon after midnight. Emergency services are now at the scene and are ensuring that no one is left in the building, trapped under the rubble.

(b) It was all very traditional. The big top, an enormous, striped, canvas thing, was pitched in a car-park and, inside, the wooden benches rose in tiers round the sawdust-filled ring. The high wire was fixed across the top and various bits of equipment were placed outside the ring ready for use, a trampoline, spring-boards and so on. When everyone had taken their seats, the band struck up and the master of ceremonies in his top hat and tails made his entrance.

(c) At the gates there were crowds of pickets being held back by police. Anyone who went in had to run the gauntlet of jeers, catcalls and shouts of 'scab, scab, scab'. Inside, the machines stood idle and the management held meetings to discuss whether to take a hard line, to submit the dispute to arbitration, to appease the work-force with an acceptable compromise or simply to cave in and meet all demands.

(d) The jurors filed in and took their places without a glance at the dock, where Smith stood passively. The opposing counsel, their work done, tidied their briefs, smoothed their gowns and put away their books. In the public gallery they talked in low tones. The ushers stood silently at their posts. Then the clerk of the court rose to his feet and cleared his throat …

(e) The procession moved down the main shopping street chanting slogans, each group behind its leaders, who carried banners and placards. There had been isolated scuffles but, on the whole, the stewards did their job well and onlookers were impressed by the orderliness of the occasion. When the marchers reached the square, they spread out in front of the platform, on either side of which loudspeakers were directed out towards the footsore crowds.

Description

People's Appearance

Complete each passage below with the correct words from the list above it to make an accurate description of one of the people in the illustration.

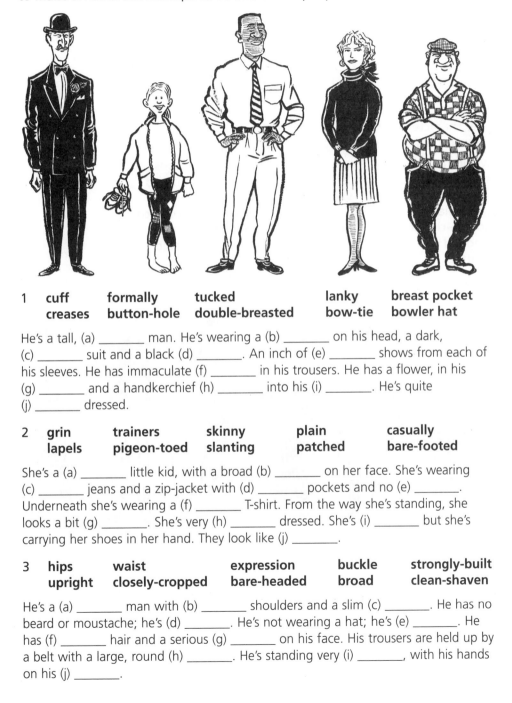

1 **cuff**   **formally**   **tucked**   **lanky**   **breast pocket**
   creases   **button-hole**   **double-breasted**   **bow-tie**   **bowler hat**

He's a tall, (a) _____ man. He's wearing a (b) _____ on his head, a dark,
(c) _____ suit and a black (d) _____. An inch of (e) _____ shows from each of
his sleeves. He has immaculate (f) _____ in his trousers. He has a flower, in his
(g) _____ and a handkerchief (h) _____ into his (i) _____. He's quite
(j) _____ dressed.

2 **grin**   **trainers**   **skinny**   **plain**   **casually**
   lapels   **pigeon-toed**   **slanting**   **patched**   **bare-footed**

She's a (a) _____ little kid, with a broad (b) _____ on her face. She's wearing
(c) _____ jeans and a zip-jacket with (d) _____ pockets and no (e) _____.
Underneath she's wearing a (f) _____ T-shirt. From the way she's standing, she
looks a bit (g) _____. She's very (h) _____ dressed. She's (i) _____ but she's
carrying her shoes in her hand. They look like (j) _____.

3 **hips**   **waist**   **expression**   **buckle**   **strongly-built**
   upright   **closely-cropped**   **bare-headed**   **broad**   **clean-shaven**

He's a (a) _____ man with (b) _____ shoulders and a slim (c) _____. He has no
beard or moustache; he's (d) _____. He's not wearing a hat; he's (e) _____. He
has (f) _____ hair and a serious (g) _____ on his face. His trousers are held up by
a belt with a large, round (h) _____. He's standing very (i) _____, with his hands
on his (j) _____.

4

bow	clasped	slender	wavy	parted
teens	polo-neck	figure	pleated	high-heeled

She's young, still in her (a) _____. She has a (b) _____ (c) _____ and she's standing with her hands (d) _____ in front of her. Her fair, (e) _____ hair, which is (f) _____ in the middle, has a ribbon with a (g) _____ in it. She's wearing a full, knee-length (h) _____ skirt, a loose (i) _____ pullover and black, (j) _____ shoes.

5

folded	obese	baggy	braces	thirtyish
checked	rolled up	side-burns	flat cap	bow-legged

He's not very old, maybe (a) _____, and he's standing with his arms (b) _____. He's rather (c) _____, as jockeys sometimes are, and he's fat, almost (d) _____. He has a (e) _____ on, so you can't see his hair, except for his long (f) _____. He's wearing a (g) _____ shirt with the sleeves (h) _____ and a pair of (i) _____ trousers held up by (j) _____.

6 Write a brief description of each person below, referring to his or her age, character, hair, build, clothes and posture. Use any of the words from the exercises above and any of the following words which may be suitable.

wellingtons	epaulettes	beret	tousled
single-breasted	cleft chin	slim	flared
knock-kneed	waistcoat	lean	stout
spectacles	cardigan	singlet	paunch
double-chinned	top hat	shorts	frail
stooped	striped	curly	bald
spotted			

Diagrams

The exercises below give practice in comprehension of expressions which indicate position, shape and size. Draw accurately the diagrams described.

Example: From the mid-point of a vertical broken line, a dotted line extends horizontally to the right. This line is twice the length of the vertical line.

Answer:

(a) A capital 'E' is the wrong way round. Its middle horizontal extends (to the left) so that it is three times as long as each of the other horizontals.

(b) A square has a wavy line for its upper side. The top right-hand corner of the square is connected to the centre of the square with a straight diagonal line.

(c) The basic shape is a rectangle with the vertical sides twice as long as the horizontals. A wavy diagonal line connects the top right-hand corner of the rectangle with the bottom left-hand corner. In the right angle of the lower triangle thus formed is a small capital 'A' upside-down. Above the top horizontal, near the left-hand end, is a capital 'S' the wrong way round. From the centre of the right-hand vertical line, a dotted horizontal line extends to the right, the same length as each of the other horizontals, linking with the mid-point of a third vertical line which stands parallel to the other two and of the same length. A straight broken line joins the top end of this vertical line with the bottom right-hand corner of the rectangle, making it parallel with the wavy line.

Write descriptions, like those above, of the following diagrams.

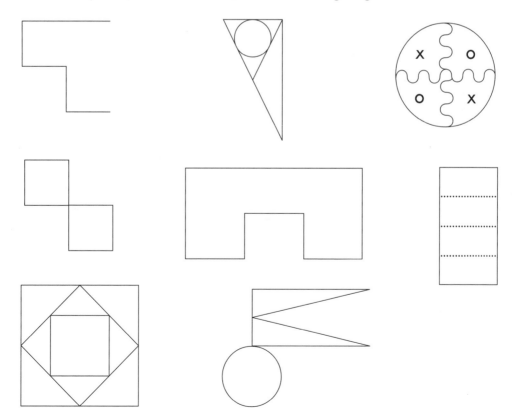

Plans

The exercises below give practice in comprehension of common expressions of position, shape and size. Draw accurately each plan described.

Example: My armchair faces the television set, which has a round vase on it in the middle and a small clock on the right of the vase. Immediately to the left of the armchair, as you sit in it, is an oval table with its greater length parallel to the arms of the chair.

Answer:

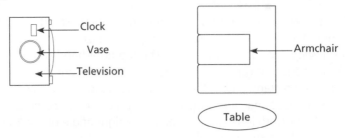

(a) My rectangular desk is about half as wide as it is long and I sit at the left-hand end of one of the longer sides on a chair with a curved back. The telephone is on my right and my business diary is in the corner furthest from me. My typewriter is in the middle of the left-hand half of the desk.

(b) The park is triangular in shape with the entrance in the middle of the longest side, facing the right-angle corner of the park. To the left as you go in, in the corner, is a round pond with four benches equally spaced round it. A straight path goes right, at an angle, from inside the entrance to a statue of Queen Victoria which stands in the middle of the side facing the pond. On either side of the statue a row of trees extends to the corners of the park.

(c) The postage stamp is square and has a vertical line from top to bottom a quarter of the way in from the right-hand side. Taking up most of the rectangle on the left is a picture of the head of President Kennedy, facing left, below which, in the bottom left-hand corner, is printed 'USA'. The price of the stamp, fifty cents, is printed in capital letters at the foot of the right-hand strip, the words one above the other, the letters about half the height of 'USA'.

(d) The room is square with the door in the middle of one wall. The window is opposite the door and takes up one-third of the length of the wall. Below the window and up against the wall is a square writing-table the same length as the window, with a chair at it so that I can look out of the window as I work. My single bed is against the wall to the right as you enter, i.e. it is at right angles to the wall with the door in it. The head of the bed is against the door-wall, so I can see the sky through the window when I wake up, and the bed is just over half the length of the wall. There is just enough room between the bed and the door for a small bed-side table. In the corner to the right of the window is a wash-basin. Between this and the bed is a small wardrobe. My armchair faces the centre of the room from the corner diametrically opposite the wash-basin, i.e. on the left as you enter the room. A book-case stands against the wall facing the wardrobe, and I have a hi-fi set next to it in the corner left of the window.

Write descriptions, like those above, of the following plans.

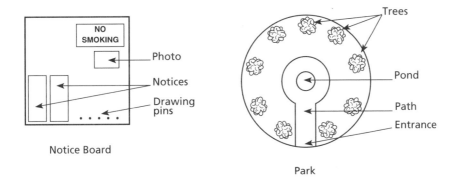

Notice Board

Park

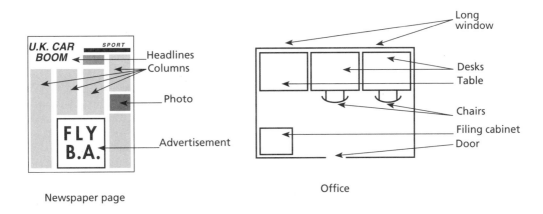

Newspaper page

Office

LETTER PHRASES

Some idiomatic phrases feature letters. What do the following mean?

Have you got an **A to Z?**
I'll have to watch my **p's and q's.**
She **drops her h's.**
We were taught **the three R's.**

Maps

The exercises below give practice in comprehension of basic geographical expressions of position and direction. Draw and mark accurately the places and features described.

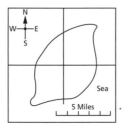

Example: The town of X is at the southernmost tip of the island, from which a road follows the coast to Y, a town halfway along the south-east coast. From Y a path rises to the peak of Mount Z in the centre of the island. Immediately to the north of Mount Z and two miles inland is an old castle. Two miles off X to the south-west is a light-house.

Answer:

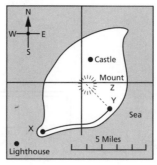

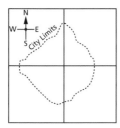

(a) In the centre of the city is the National Assembly, from where Independence Avenue goes straight to the station, at the northernmost point of the city. South of the National Assembly is People's Park, rectangular in shape and extending north to south almost to the southern limits of the city. The park is overlooked by a row of Government Ministry buildings which run alongside it on the east. Just to the west of the city is the University. Equidistant from the National Assembly, the station and the University is the Presidential Palace, just inside the city boundary. It is reached by a straight road which branches off to the left from Independence Avenue just north of the National Assembly.

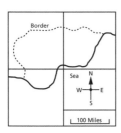

(b) The capital, A, is in the centre of the broad western part of the country, and the Vaz Mountains surround it in a rough semi-circle about 20 miles away, from west to north-east. These mountains continue eastwards along the middle of the narrower part of the country for about 100 miles parallel to the coast. On the coast, south-west of A, is the port of B, which is linked to the gold mines 20 miles inland to the north by a straight road. The country's only railway goes east from A, reaches the coast after about 50 miles and follows the coast as far as the town of C, which is at the country's easternmost extremity. The town of D is half-way along the railway between A and C, and 30 miles off it is Green Island, more or less circular in shape and linked with the mainland only by air to a small airport just north-east of D.

Describe the places and features of the maps on the left below, of an island, a city and a country, in the same way as in the previous exercises, assuming the outlines are given, as on the right.

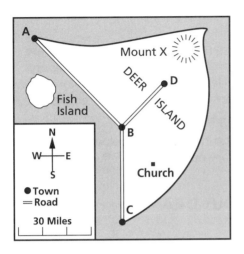
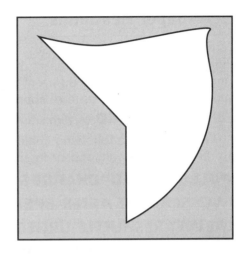

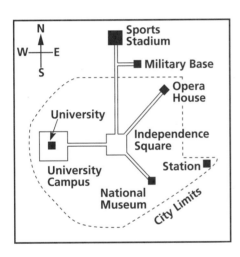
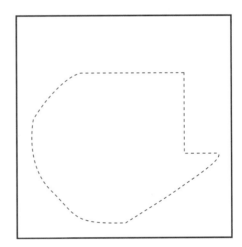

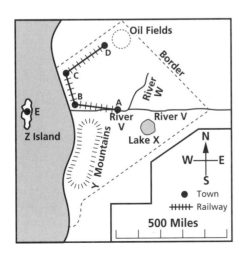
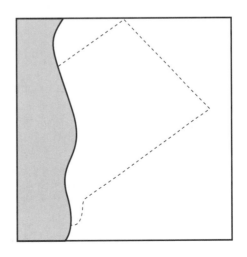

Style

Newspaper Headlines

Certain words are used very often in newspaper headlines because they are short or sound dramatic. Some of these words are not common in ordinary language or are used in a different sense. Headlines also omit certain words and use colloquial expressions, abbreviations and different verb tenses,

e.g. **STAR TO WED** (A film star is going to get married).

1   For each of the following headlines find the sentence below which expresses it as it would appear in an ordinary news announcement.

'POLLS RIGGED' CHARGES

TWO SOUGHT AFTER BREAK-OUT DRAMA

CABINET RESHUFFLE URGED

SERVICE CHIEFS GAGGED: TWO QUIT

GEMS HAUL SEIZED IN SWOOP

(a)   Allegations have been made that election results were falsified.
(b)   Police raided a house today and took possession of jewellery stolen in a recent robbery.
(c)   Police are hunting two men who made a daring escape from prison by helicopter.
(d)   Senior officers of the armed forces have been instructed not to talk to the media and, as a result, two of them have resigned.
(e)   Strong appeals have been made to the Prime Minister to make changes in his ministers.

2   Match each of the following words from the headlines above with its meaning below.

CHIEF   DRAMA   RESHUFFLE   GAG   GEMS   SEEK/SOUGHT

SWOOP   POLL(S)   QUIT   RIG   HAUL

(a)   jewels
(b)   goods stolen in robbery or taken by police or customs
(c)   to falsify
(d)   director, high-ranking officer or official
(e)   raid, to raid
(f)   to look for, ask for, want
(g)   to silence, censor, censorship
(h)   exciting, dramatic event
(i)   election, voting, public opinion survey
(j)   to rearrange, rearrangement (of senior jobs)
(k)   to resign, leave

3   Express each of the following headlines as it would appear in an ordinary news announcement.

(a) **EDITORS URGE END TO PRESS GAG**

(b) **INDIA SEEKS US AID**

(c) **GEM SMUGGLERS CAUGHT IN PORT SWOOP**

(d) **BANK RAID CASH HAUL FOUND: 3 CHARGED**

(e) **HEAD QUITS OVER 'RIGGED' EXAM RESULTS**

(f) **RAIL CHIEFS RESHUFFLED AFTER BIG LOSSES**

(g) **GOVT DEFEATED IN POLL DRAMA**

4   For each of the following words, all frequently used in headlines, find the meaning in the list below. It will help you if you look to see how they are used in the headlines at the foot of the exercise. Then express each headline as it would appear in an ordinary news announcement.

MOVE	CLASH	WOO	BID	FOIL	HALT
OUST	QUIZ	PLEA	BAN	BACK	FLEE

(a) to prevent
(b) strong request, call for help, appeal
(c) attempt, to attempt
(d) stop, to stop
(e) to prohibit, prohibition
(f) fighting, argument, conflict, to argue, to fight
(g) support, to support
(h) to force out of office, remove from high position
(i) run away from, escape
(j) to try to attract
(k) action, step, to take action
(l) to question, interrogate

(a) **DICTATOR OUSTED: PLEA FOR CALM**

(b) **NEW MOVES TO HALT BORDER CLASHES**

(c) GOVT BACKS ARMS BAN TO WOO LEFT

(d) **KIDNAP BID FOILED: 3 QUIZZED, 2 FLEE**

AMERICAN ENGLISH 3

The following words are given with American spelling. What is the British spelling?

gray	pajamas	center	quarreling
labor	airplane	dialog	check (bank)
ax	favorite	defense	neighbor
plow	pretense	theater	signaled
color	kidnaped	catalog	traveler

5　Instructions as above.

SPLIT　LEAK　RIDDLE　PROBE　AXE　LIFT
CURB　BAFFLED　STORM　RAP　CALL　ENVOY

(a)　mystery
(b)　to escape, escape (of secret information)
(c)　diplomat, ambassador
(d)　close, dismiss, cancel, closure, dismissal
(e)　remove (restrictions, prohibitions)
(f)　criticise, reprimand
(g)　at a loss to explain, mystified
(h)　restrict, restriction
(i)　divide, division
(j)　investigate, investigation
(k)　to demand, to appeal, demand, appeal
(l)　angry argument

(a)　**CABINET LEAK: CALL FOR PROBE**
(b)　**EU SPLIT OVER LIFTING OF TRAVEL CURBS**
(c)　**DEAD ENVOY RIDDLE: YARD BAFFLED**
(d)　**PM RAPS BBC IN JOBS AXE STORM**

6　Make brief headlines from the following news stories.
(a)　Eighteen people were killed when the army tried to overthrow the government.
(b)　A leading diplomat has been mysteriously murdered.
(c)　The Prime Minister is trying to win the support of the coal miners' trade unions.
(d)　The director of British Petroleum has been forced to resign.
(e)　A Member of Parliament was questioned by the police in an investigation into the use of illegal drugs.

7　Express the following headlines in ordinary English.

(a)　**PEER DIES IN FLATS BLAZE DRAMA**

(b)　**BLAST TOLL RISING: WITNESSES SOUGHT**

(c)　**COMMONS STORM OVER DEFENCE CUTS**

(d)　**M-WAY DEATH CRASH: BRITON HELD**

ORIGINS OF PLACE NAMES

'Oxford' means 'the shallow river crossing (ford) used by oxen'. 'Cambridge' simply means 'bridge on the River Cam'. Not all place names are so easily explained but a list of common endings will help:

bourne, burn (spring, stream)	Eastbourne, Blackburn
burgh, bury (fortified town)	Edinburgh, Canterbury
cester, chester (Roman fort, 'castra')	Gloucester, Manchester
ham (home village)	Petersham, Birmingham
mouth (river mouth)	Bournemouth, Plymouth
ton (farm, village, town)	Brighton, Bolton
wich, wick (dwelling, farm, village)	Greenwich, Gatwick
minster (monastery, church)	Axminster, Westminster

Formal English

1   Certain established phrases are used repeatedly in the language of forms, travel conditions, regulations, advertisements and notices. Rewrite each of the following in simple English as if you were explaining the meaning to someone.

E.g. Not transferable. (rail ticket)
No one else is allowed to use this ticket.

Parental consent required if under 16. (holiday conditions)
Children under 16 must have their parents' permission.

(a)   Subject to alteration. (timetable)
(b)   For further information see over. (timetable)
(c)   To be retained and produced on request. (rail ticket)
(d)   Enter maiden name, if applicable. (official form)
(e)   This portion to be given up. (theatre ticket)
(f)   Complete and detach bottom section. (bank form)
(g)   Affix recent photograph here. (application form)
(h)   Liable to alteration without notice. (timetable)
(i)   See notes overleaf. (passport application form)
(j)   Insert correct amount only. (notice on automatic machine)
(k)   All offers subject to availability. (chain-store gift catalogue)
(l)   Services in bold type convey sleeping-cars only. (rail timetable)
(m)   Delete where applicable. (official form)
(n)   Enquire within. (notice in shop window)
(o)   Special rates available for parties. (theatre conditions)
(p)   Not valid on underground train services unless specifically stated. (travel ticket)
(q)   Indicate marital status by ticking appropriate box. (official form)
(r)   Non-refundable deposit payable at time of reservation. (travel agent's conditions)
(s)   Expiry date. (one-week travel ticket)
(t)   Insert full name of spouse. (official form)

2   Rewrite each of the following in simple English as if you were explaining it to someone.

E.g. You will be asked to show that adequate funds will be available to meet the cost of fees, your own maintenance and that of any dependants during your stay. (immigration regulations for students studying in Britain)

They'll ask you to show that you will have enough money to pay your college fees and to support yourself and any other members of your family you bring with you.

(a)   Should there be any defect in this appliance, consult the supplier. (note with washing machine)
(b)   Follow the instructions on the reverse of the form. (official form)
(c)   No liability can be accepted for events beyond our control. (travel firm's rules)
(d)   It should be noted that possession of the minimum entrance requirements does not guarantee admission. (university entrance regulations)
(e)   Should you wish to extend your rental beyond the agreed terminating date, it is imperative that the renting station is advised immediately. (car hire conditions)

(f) Normally the bank asks for seven days' notice of any withdrawals from a Deposit Account, but in emergencies you can draw immediately. (bank conditions)

(g) You will receive four tickets. Should you require more books than this at any time, extra tickets will be issued on demand. (library rules)

(h) Possession of such a letter is not obligatory but should greatly facilitate entry. (immigration regulations)

(i) The renter is responsible for the first £45 of each and every accident involving any damage to or loss of the vehicle during the renting period. The renter's liability may be waived by payment of a collision damage waiver fee at the rate of 95p per day. (car hire insurance rules)

3   The information below is given as if spoken informally. Rewrite each item as it would appear formally in the notice, form, printed regulations etc. indicated in brackets. Suggested beginnings are given for the first few items.

E.g. You've got to understand that we accept students only if they've got permission to study from the Home Office. (college regulations)

Students should be aware that they will be admitted to the college strictly on condition that they have obtained leave to study from the Home Office.

(a) If you want to complain, you must write a letter to the tour operator. (travel conditions)
Any complaints should be ...

(b) If you buy anything during the sale, we won't give you your money back if you later decide you don't want it (shop notice)
We regret that no refunds ...

(c) If, by chance, there's a fire, don't panic. Just leave quietly. The exits are marked on the plan at the bottom of the notice. (notice in public hall)
In the event of ...

(d) You should go to, or phone, your embassy if you have any problems. (advice for travellers)
Travellers are advised ...

(e) Please don't smoke. (notice in cinema)
Patrons are ...

(f) It's cheaper if you get a Certificate of Posting when you actually post your letter (the counter clerk will fill it in). You can get one later but it's more expensive. (Post Office regulations)

(g) These arrangements may have to be changed, particularly if the weather's bad. (travel conditions)

(h) Please keep this receipt. You may have to show it later on. (official receipt)

(i) The firm can't promise to send the goods you order until you send them the whole price.(business letter)

(j) If you want a Certificate of Attendance, you'll have to show your Admission Slip. It's not absolutely necessary for you to have a teacher's note saying you come regularly, but it'll make things a lot easier. (college rules)

English in Advertising

Trade Names

1   Many firms and shops choose a short name which attracts attention, is easy to remember and immediately identifies the service being offered. This name is often spelt in a kind of simple phonetic spelling to make it even more unique and memorable, e.g. EAZIWASH (easy wash) is a launderette and FIZZEEK (physique) is a gymnasium and health club.

Below are the real names of fourteen firms or shops. Give the normal spelling of each and find on the right the kind of business it is.

(a)	LITE BITE	photo-processing shop
(b)	SHUSELLA	photo-copying firm
(c)	KEEP-A-KREASE	children's clothes shop
(d)	SUPASNAPS	snack bar
(e)	KWICK KOPY	shoe-shop
(f)	KWALITY FASHIONS	dry-cleaners
(g)	KUMFY KIDDY WEAR	taxi firm
(h)	HANDICARS	garage and repair shop
(i)	MR KLEEN	women's clothes shop
(j)	SNAX	dry cleaners
(k)	MOTOR KARE	hairdressers
(l)	LOOKRITE	snack bar
(m)	FLITE CENTRE	car-hire firm
(n)	U-DRIVE	travel agency

2   Products are often named in the same way as the businesses above. Give the normal spelling of each real product below and write down the kind of product you think it is.

(a)	KLEENOFF	(c)	ANSAFONE	(e)	KARRIMOR
(b)	KATTOMEAT	(d)	RESTRITE	(f)	ANSADOR

3   Some firms use normal spelling in their names but form them by combining two words into one. What kind of business do the following real firms do?

(a)	TRANSLAGENCY	(d)	SECURICOR	(g)	SUNTOURS
(b)	AUTOCHECK	(e)	QUICK-LETS	(h)	DATAFLOW
(c)	AUTOPASS	(f)	FIGURETRIM	(i)	FINNAIR

Puns

A pun is a humorous use of a word or phrase which has two meanings or of two words or phrases which look or sound similar. Puns are used not only in jokes but in many forms of publicity because they catch the eye and amuse. Explain the following puns by giving the two possible meanings (often one meaning is literal and the other figurative).

E.g.: **WHEN YOU DECIDE TO GIVE HER A RING, GIVE US A RING**
(Advertisement for a jeweller's shop)

Explanation: 'to give someone a ring' means, literally, 'to give a wedding or engagement ring', or figuratively, 'to telephone'.

(a) **FOR A FEW POUNDS YOU CAN LOSE A FEW**
(Advertisement for a slimming course)

(b) **GO UP IN THE WORLD**
(Advertisement to recruit air stewards and stewardesses)

(c) **WE'LL GIVE YOU SOUND ADVICE**
(Hi-fi shop advertisement)

(d) **HAVE YOU THOUGHT ABOUT BUYING OUR NEW BED? SLEEP ON IT** (Advertisement for a new bed)

(e) **IT'S NOT WORTH DYING FOR A DRINK**
(Advertisement warning of the dangers of alcoholism)

(f) **MAKE A SNAP DECISION**
(Advertisement for a new camera)

(g) **IT'S GOOD FOR YOU, NATURALLY**
(Advertisement for fruit juice)

(h) **GO BY AIR. IT'S PLANE COMMON SENSE**
(Advertisement for air travel)

(i) *WE'LL GIVE YOU RED-CARPET TREATMENT (OR BLUE, OR GREEN, OR BROWN, OR YELLOW...)*
(Carpet shop advertisement)

(j) **SEA FOR YOURSELF**
(Advertisement to attract recruits to the Royal Navy)

(k) **TRY OUR GLUE ONCE AND YOU'LL ALWAYS STICK WITH US**
(Advertisement for a brand of glue)

(l) **THE WEATHER-MEN CAN'T GUARANTEE YOU AN INDIAN SUMMER, BUT WE CAN**
(Travel agency advertisement)

(m) **WE'LL GIVE YOU FOOD FOR THOUGHT**
(Restaurant advertisement)

Spoken English

Forms of Spoken Address

How do British people address each other? What do they call each other?
Complete the spoken phrases at the end of each sentence below with a word
or phrase from the following list. In some cases two or even three items
could be used. If no particular form of address is normally used, write
nothing. Some of the words in the list are used more than once, and some
are not used in any of the phrases.

E.g. Department store assistant to woman customer: Can I help you, _____?
Answer: madam

Parents to their child: What are you doing, _____?
Answer: dear, love or darling

Rail traveller to ticket-clerk: Return to Lancaster, please, _____.
Answer: nothing

grandma	daddy	viewers	ladies and gentlemen	mate
caller	dear	Your Majesty	officer	dad
mum	men	listeners	men and women	madam
mister	sir	grannie	gentleman	grandpa
grandad	love	my friend	darling	mummy

(a) Child to his or her mother: Can I go out, _____?
(b) Telephone operator: Please hold the line, _____.
(c) Television presenter to people watching at home: Welcome to the Saturday
     Night Show, _____.
(d) Child to his or her grandfather: Thank you for the present, _____.
(e) Someone to a bank-clerk or librarian: Can you help me, _____?
(f) Someone making a formal speech to his audience: I'll try to be brief, _____.
(g) Polite shop-assistant to male customer: Can I help you, _____?
(h) Someone to the Queen: Good evening, _____.
(i) Customer to a shop-assistant: Can I try on this coat, _____?
(j) Wife to her husband: You look tired, _____.
(k) Radio presenter to people at home: Now we have a surprise for you, _____.
(l) Workman to a man passing by: What's the time, _____?
(m) Policeman to a man who asks for help: Yes, _____.
(n) Policeman to a woman who asks for help: Yes, _____.
(o) Someone to a policeman: Excuse me, _____.
(p) Child to his or her grandmother: Here are your glasses, _____.
(q) Woman shopkeeper in a small, friendly shop to a customer: What would you
     like, _____?
(r) Soldier to his commanding officer: Can I go, _____?
(s) Commanding officer to his soldiers: I want more effort, _____.
(t) Child to his or her father: Goodnight, _____.
(u) Someone to a stranger in the street: Excuse me, _____.

Colloquial Responses

On the right in the exercises below are some common colloquial responses, i.e. phrases often used in particular, informal situations. Of course, different people respond in different ways, but the phrases below are very common.

1   For each spoken item on the left below find the most natural response on the right.

(a) You mustn't tell a soul.	Dump it anywhere.
(b) Where shall I put your case?	Care for a spin?
(c) Can I bring a friend to your party?	My lips are sealed.
(d) People say you're very generous.	Flattery will get you nowhere.
(e) I like your new car.	The more the merrier.

2   Instructions as above.

(a) How did you know I was going out with Jenny?	Well, boys will be boys.
(b) I thought you were going to accept the offer.	Beggars can't be choosers.
(c) Bobby's in trouble at school.	I'm having second thoughts.
(d) I'm afraid this is the only job I can offer you.	Well, you can't win them all.
(e) I didn't get the job.	A little bird told me.

3   Instructions as above.

(a) How shall we decide?	I'm afraid I haven't a clue.
(b) I've got a coin.	Let's toss for it.
(c) Do you know where the cinema is?	Let me sleep on it.
(d) We need a decision soon.	Oh, it's on the tip of my tongue.
(e) Do you know what it's called?	OK. You toss, I'll call. Tails!

4   Instructions as above.

(a) Cheers!	I could do with one.
(b) Can I have some more meat?	Oh, this is on me.
(c) I'll buy the drinks.	Help yourself.
(d) Cup of tea?	Cheers!
(e) I don't think I can afford this restaurant. It looks a bit expensive.	No, it's my round.

5   Instructions as above.

(a) Can I use your phone?	Yes, by the skin of my teeth.
(b) Our plan's a failure. It won't work.	If you don't mind taking pot luck.
(c) Did you catch the train?	Every little helps.
(d) Can I come to lunch?	Back to square one.
(e) Sorry I can't make a bigger donation.	Be my guest.

6   Instructions as above.

(a) I've got some news.	OK. Thanks all the same.
(b) I hope the weather's good for our trip tomorrow.	Well, It can't be helped.
(c) He's a very odd chap.	I'm all ears.
(d) I've left our tickets at home!	It takes all sorts.
(e) Sorry I can't help you.	I'm keeping my fingers crossed.

In the following exercises, the situations are very informal, e.g. between very close friends, when we sometimes use very casual, ironic or even rude responses.

7   Instructions as above.
(a) Can you lend me £100?   Serves you right.
(b) I've eaten too much. I feel ill.   OK. Suit yourself.
(c) Where were you last night?   That'll be the day.
(d) I think I'd rather go to a pub.   You must be joking.
(e) I'll pay you back soon.   Mind your own business.

8   Instructions as above.
(a) Why don't you do some work?   Have it your own way.
(b) I insist on doing it like this.   How should I know?
(c) Where's Ann tonight?   I like that!
(d) I've borrowed your coat.   Rather you than me.
(e) It's very cold, but I'm going for a walk. I can't be bothered.

Exclamations

1   People often react to certain situations by using sounds rather than real words, and people from different countries often use different sounds, e.g. British people often say 'ouch!' when they feel a sudden pain, whereas other nationalities sometimes say 'aie!' Of course different British people will have different responses, but the following are common.

Answer the questions below with sounds from the following list.

giddyup!   mm!   eh? (rhymes with 'say')   wow! (rhymes with 'how')
whoah!   sh!   ' boo! (rhymes with 'too')   there, there
whoops!   well?

What do you say if you ...
(a) ... want someone to be quiet?
(b) ... don't catch what a friend says?
(c) ... want a horse to start or go faster?
(d) ... comfort a child in pain and crying?
(e) ... jump out from behind a tree to surprise someone?
(f) ... suddenly lose your balance, or drop something?
(g) ... are waiting for someone to answer your question?
(h) ... are suddenly impressed by something?
(i) ... want a horse to slow down or stop?
(j) ... express spontaneous delight!

2   Instructions as above.

hear, hear   er (rhymes with 'sir')   gosh!
now, now   hi! (rhymes with 'lie')   ta-ta
cheers   oi! (rhymes with 'boy')   ta

What do you say if you ...
(a) ... thank a friend casually?
(b) ... hesitate or forget something?
(c) ... calm an over-excited, angry friend?
(d) ... and a friend raise your glasses to drink together?
(e) ... say goodbye casually to a friend?
(f) ... express your agreement with something said in a speech?
(g) ... greet a friend casually?
(h) ... see someone trying to steal your bag?
(i) ... express surprise?

Spoken Numbers and Measurements

1   The sentences below are written as they would be spoken. Rewrite them
as they would normally be written, using numbers and abbreviated forms.

E.g. I take a size fourteen and a half shirt.
    I take a size 14½ shirt.

Ten per cent of the working population earn less than six thousand, five
hundreds pounds a year.
10% of the working population earn less than £6,500 a year.

(a) Forty minus fifteen plus six is thirty-one.
(b) Eighty-one divided by three is twenty-seven.
(c) Three times six is eighteen.
(d) Queen Elizabeth the First reigned from fifteen fifty-eight to sixteen oh three.
(e) The show is due to commence at seven thirty p.m. on the second of August.
(f) It cost me six pounds seventy-five pence.
(g) Phone me any time on four double-one four eight five oh.
(h) Please note that our reference number is double-four dash seven stroke five oh
     nine.
(i) The total cost is estimated at two million, four hundred and seventy-one
     thousand, eight hundred and fifty pounds.
(j) The mixture is two thirds water.
(k) A litre is one point seven six pints.
(l) Twenty-two per cent of the candidates passed with distinction.
(m) The temperature was thirty degrees centigrade, that is eighty-six degrees
     fahrenheit.
(n) It measures four feet two and three quarter inches by two feet eight and a half
     inches.
(o) France beat England three nil. (football)
(p) Brazil and Italy drew three all. (football)
(q) The score stands at thirty love to Becker. (tennis)

2   Write out the following sentences exactly as they would be spoken, i.e.
as in the exercise above.
(a) $73 + 20 - 43 = 50$
(b) $129 \div 3 = 43$
(c) $4 \times 21 = 84$
(d) Edward VII died in 1910.

(e) It was exactly 11.35 a.m. on 21st May.

(f) They cost £3.25 each.

(g) Our new phone number is 307 2201.

(h) Please quote reference no. 8/2-771.

(i) The population is 3,255,840.

(j) I am ⅛ French.

(k) 1 mile = 1.609 kilometres.

(l) It is 17.38% gold.

(m) Water freezes at 32°F, i.e. 0 °C.

(n) The picture measured 2'6 ½" x 5' 8 ¼".

(o) We won 3:0. (football)

(p) The final score was 2:2. (football)

(q) The score's 15:0 to me at the moment. (tennis)

Well-Known Spoken Phrases

The following common phrases are associated with particular situations. Identify each phrase by describing briefly who would say it and in what circumstances.

E.g. 'Please fasten your safety-belts.'
    Air-stewardess to passengers before take-off or landing.

(a) 'Mind the doors!'

(b) 'To eat here or take away?'

(c) 'Many happy returns.'

(d) 'How do you plead?'

(e) 'Just a trim, please.'

(f) 'Have you anything to declare?'

(g) 'Heel!'

(h) 'Take this prescription and come back and see me in a week.'

(i) 'I'm putting you through.'

(j) 'A pint of bitter, please.'

(k) 'Going … going … gone!'

(l) 'Here's to the bride and groom.'

(m) 'I now pronounce you man and wife.'

(n) 'I swear to tell the truth, the whole truth and nothing but the truth.'

(o) 'This won't hurt.'

(p) 'God bless her and all who sail in her.'

(q) 'Amen.'

(r) 'Once upon a time …'

(s) 'Say "Cheese".'

(t) 'All aboard!'

(u) 'Man overboard!'

Colloquial English and Slang

The kind of informal English which is normal in ordinary conversation but is not considered acceptable in more formal language is called 'colloquial'. 'Slang' is even more informal language and consists mainly of particular words and phrases used principally by one group of people, e.g. young children, teenagers, students, professional people, working people etc. (The line between colloquial and slang words is not at all clear and many words considered colloquial by some people would be considered slang by others). After each conversation below, rewrite the conversation with the colloquial or slang item in a more formal style.

E.g. Alan: *Do you fancy* going to the *pictures tonight?*
 Jill: *Great. Hang on*, though. There's something good on *telly.*

 Answer:
 Alan: Would you like to go the cinema this evening?
 Jill: Wonderful. But wait. There's a good programme on television.

1 Peter: Lend *us* a few *quid.* I'm *broke.*
 Tony: Here's a *fiver.*
 Peter: *Smashing. Ta.*

2 George: Where's my *thingumajig?*
 Eileen: *Whatsisname's* got it.

3 Chris: Do you like your new school?
 Gus: It's *OK.*
 Chris: And the *kids* in your class?
 Gus: They're a *decent bunch.*
 Chris: And the teacher?
 Gus: Oh, he's a *terrific bloke.*

4 Fred: I'm *not too keen* on this new *guy* in the office.
 Alex: *Yeah,* he's a bit of a *big-head. Throws his weight around.*
 Fred: *Yeah,* if I get any more *hassle* from him, I'm going to tell him what I think.
 Alex: *Come off it.* You haven't got the *guts.* You'd *get the sack.*

5 Joe: *Posh* suit!
 Brian: My grandparents' 50th wedding anniversary. We're having a bit of a *do.*
 Joe: Come and have a drink first. *On me.*
 Brian: Just for a *mo.* Mustn't get there *plastered.*

6 Mr Stanton: You look a bit *fed up.* What's up?
 Mr Moore: Someone's *pinched* my *brolly* and it's *coming down in buckets.*
 Mr Stanton: Oh, *tough luck.*

7 Valerie: Saw a film the other night. *Chap falls for* a girl, then discovers she's dying. Bit of a *tear-jerker.* I suppose it was pretty *corny,* but I liked it. Mary Major had a part in it. She must be *pushing* 70.

8 Bob: I think my *old banger's clapped out*. I'll have to get a new one.
 Jim: Yes, it does look *past it.* What'll you get?
 Bob: I rather *fancy* the new Rover.
 Jim: *Classy!* It'll cost you a *packet.*

9   Donald: Someone's *walked off* with my *specs*!
     Sheila: Don't be *daft.* You've got them in your hand.
     Donald: Oh, yes. I'm going *bonkers.*

10   Ann: I'm afraid the new secretary's *a dead loss*, Joan. The red-head with the
     trendy clothes.
     Joan: You're right. She thinks she's the *cat's whiskers*, but in actual fact she's a
     bit *dim.*
     Ann: Yes, her work's poor and, as you say, she *fancies herself*. She's very
     snooty with the other staff.
     Joan: Do you think we ought to *give her the push*?
     Ann: I'm afraid so, but she'll be *shattered*.

ODD ENGLISH

Advertisements and notices can sometimes produce unintentionally amusing
results. Here are some examples.

Antique table for sale by lady with unusual legs.
Green child's bicycle for sale.
They chased two dogs in their pyjamas.
We regret to tell you that Mrs Anita Wells is recovering from a heart attack.
**Women's Club meeting 7 p.m. Tuesday. An antiques expert will give an
opinion on any unusual objects you have at home. Bring your husbands.**

Popular Language

Informal language used by people and found in the popular media is very colourful and always changing. Below is a selection.

A1, ace very good, excellent

acid trip hallucinatory experience caused by drugs

agro aggravation, bother: 'Don't give me any aggro.'

aka also known as

alternative non-conventional: alternative medicine

awesome wonderful, amazing

bad news undesirable person who causes trouble: 'She's bad news.'

bag interest, taste, favourite activity: 'Opera isn't my bag.'

beats me I can't understand why...

bend one's ear bore one by talking continuously

berk fool, stupid person

bottle courage: 'He's got no bottle.'

bug irritate: 'It bugs me.'

chat up get into conversation with, usually member of opposite sex

clout (n) influence: 'They won't listen to me. I've got no clout.'

cool fashionable

cop-out (v/n) avoid(ance of) a situation 'That's a cop-out. Answer the question properly.'

crash out go to sleep

creep unpleasant person

don't want to know have no interest: 'Drugs? No thanks, I don't want to know.'

dosh money

downside the negative points about a situation

drag (n) bore, nuisance: 'I've got to do my homework. What a drag!'

eco- (prefix) ecological

fab fabulous, wonderful

flap (v/n) panic: 'He's flapping.' 'He's in a flap.'

flexible friend credit card

flog sell

freak fanatic, enthusiast

freak out react very emotionally: 'She freaked out when I told her the news.'

-free (suffix): free of, not containing, e.g. sugar-/cholesterol-/nuclear-free

get lost! go away!

ghetto blaster powerful portable radio/cassette/CD player

glitz superficial glamour

glitzy (adj): 'The Oscar Award Ceremony is a glitzy occasion.'

go ape lose control, get excited, angry: 'My dad went ape when I told him I'd crashed his car.'

grab (v) appeal to: 'How does it grab you?'

grand thousand, usually money: 'It cost ten grand.' (dollars, pounds)

groupie young girl fan who follows a rock star

hang out spend time talking with friends

hooked on addicted to

iffy uncertain

in fashionable: 'in-singer', 'in-restaurant', 'in-thing'

item a romantically attached couple: 'Lyn and Steve are an item now, did you know?'

Joe Bloggs the ordinary, average person

leftie person with radical or left-wing views

like sort of, kind of, almost meaningless word indicating lack of confidence in vocabulary: 'I was, like, impressed.'

Mickey Mouse (adj) worthless, not serious:'I don't want to work for a

Mickey Mouse operation like that.'

mind-blowing amazing, verb: 'It'll blow your mind.'

mind-boggling amazing

neat good

no-no taboo, something one mustn't do or say: 'When I was young, public kissing was a no-no.'

not on out of the question, impossible

no way not at all, out of the question, no chance: 'There's no way I'm doing that again!'

o.d *(v)* to take an overdose of drugs, or to have too much of something: 'He o.d.ed and was taken to hospital.'

oldie old person

on a roll having a run of luck or success

one-off *(n/adj)* unique, unlike any other: a one-off person, thing, situation

out to lunch crazy, out of touch (with reality)

pig out eat a very big meal

(in) pole position favourite to win: 'In next week's election the Republican candidate is in pole position.'

prat fool, stupid person

puke *(n/v)* vomit

rave big, all-night disco party

right? often used by young people at the end of a sentence to mean 'OK?' or 'You understand?': 'I'm going, right?'

rip-off *(v/n)* to cheat/rob, a dishonest action: 'I've been ripped off.' 'The restaurant was a rip-off.'

roll-up self-made cigarette

sarnie sandwich

scene to my liking or taste: 'It's not my scene.'

schmuck fool, idiot

smashed drunk

squeaky clean morally upright and correct

sussed well-informed, streetwise: 'She's sussed.'

suss (out) work out, find out: 'I can't suss her/this out.'

switched on well-informed, efficient

TLC tender loving care: 'What he needs is some TLC.'

together *(adj)* well-balanced: 'She's a together person.'

upbeat lively, positive

upside the positive points about a situation

uptight tense, worried

veggie *(n/adj)* vegetarian

wacky eccentric, odd

wannabe one who wants to be rich, famous etc. 'He's a wannabe rock-star.'

weirdo very strange person

wet *(adj/n)* boring, weak (person)

what it's all about what the main purpose is: 'We exist to have a good time. That's what life is all about.'

wrinklie old person

yob hooligan

yonks a long time

yuck! (exclamation) (adj. **yucky**) Disgusting!

Miscellaneous

Geo-political Names

1   Explain the difference between the two names in each of the following pairs.
(a)   England and (Great) Britain
(b)   (Great) Britain and the United Kingdom
(c)   (Great) Britain and the British Isles
(d)   Europe and Continental Europe
(e)   The Middle East and the Far East
(f)   India and the Indian Subcontinent
(g)   America and North America
(h)   South America and Latin America
(i)   The Arctic and the Antarctic
(j)   Australia and Australasia
(k)   South Africa and Southern Africa

2   Explain the difference between the two adjectives in each of the following pairs.
(a)   Arab and Arabic
(b)   Scottish and Scotch
(c)   Oriental and Occidental

3   Match each country on the left below with the name on the right by which it is also known.
(a)   Holland   Eire
(b)   Iran   The Netherlands
(c)   Myanmar   Ulster
(d)   Sri Lanka   Persia
(e)   The Republic of Ireland   Ceylon
(f)   Northern Ireland   Burma

4   Which countries are referred to by the following expressions?
(a)   The European Union countries
(b)   The (British) Commonwealth
(c)   The NATO countries
(d)   The West Indies
(e)   The Gulf States
(f)   The Third World

5   Which countries are sometimes referred to by the following colloquial expressions?
(a)   The States
(b)   Down Under
(c)   The Land of the Rising Sun
(d)   The Emerald Isle

6   For each country below give i) the adjective and ii) the word describing the person who comes from that country.

e.g. China   i) Chinese   ii) A Chinese
     Poland   i) Polish   ii) A Pole
     Wales   i) Welsh   ii) a Welshman/Welshwoman

(a) Pakistan   (g) Sweden   (m) Iraq   (s) Portugal
(b) Peru   (h) New Zealand   (n) Spain   (t) France
(c) Thailand   (i) Lebanon   (o) Finland
(d) Scotland   (j) Denmark   (p) Belgium
(e) Turkey   (k) Holland   (q) Ireland
(f) Philippines   (l) England   (r) Bangladesh

7   Inhabitants of London, Cairo and Washington are called Londoners, Cairenes and Washingtonians. Of which cities are the following people inhabitants?

(a) Parisians   (e) Neapolitans   (i) Liverpudlians
(b) Chicagoans   (f) Aberdonians   (j) Viennese
(c) Venetians   (g) Milanese   (k) Muscovites
(d) Mancunians   (h) Glaswegians   (l) Romans

Names and Titles

1   Put each of the following words and phrases in its correct place in the sentences below.

surname   pen-name   maiden name
stage name   first name   hyphenated name (or 'double-barrelled name')
nickname   alias   pet name

(a) My name is Bob Jones. Of course 'Jones' is my _____.
(b) Bob, short for 'Robert', is my _____.
(c) At school the other boys called me 'Brains'. It was my _____.
(d) As a criminal I used the false name 'Fred Yates'. That was my _____.
(e) When I write novels I call myself Simon Sims. That's my _____.
(f) Some people have two parts to their family name, e.g. Mr Smith-Stewart. This is called a _____.
(g) I was Miss North before I married, so 'North' is my _____.
(h) My wife affectionately calls me 'Dimple'. It's a kind of _____.
(i) As an actress in the theatre I was known as Gloria Gold. That was my _____.

2   **Ms Louise Manners**   **W. G. Smithson Esq.**
    Mrs P. Tucker M.P.   **Sir Robin Sawyer**
    Jones Bros.   **Rev. Graham Lee**
    G. L. Cousins M.A.   **John Fox O.B.E.**
    Adm. V.E. Nott R.N. (ret) **W.P.C. Lockwood**
    Z. Wilkins R.A.   **H.R.H. The Prince of Wales**

Answer the following questions from the list of people above.
(a) Who used to be a high-ranking naval officer?
(b) Who is in the police force?
(c) Who has a university degree?
(d) Who prefers not to state whether she is married?
(e) Who is a priest?
(f) Who has received a knighthood?
(g) Who sits in the House of Commons?
(h) Who is formally addressed on an envelope?
(i) Who has a royal title?
(j) Which members of a family run a business together?
(k) Who is a recognised artist?
(l) Who has received an honour from the King or Queen?

3   Give the full names for which the following are the common short forms.

(a) Dick	(d) Bert	(g) Tom	(j) Tricia
(b) Ted	(e) Andy	(h) Bob	(k) Jenny
(c) Bill	(f) Tony	(i) Liz	(l) Maggie

Give the common short forms of the following names.

(m) James	(s) Leslie
(n) Gerald	(t) Frederick
(o) Michael	(u) Pamela
(p) Christopher	(v) Catherine
(q) Joseph	(w) Susan
(r) Harold	(x) Diana

INNOVATIONS

Social and technological innovations have brought new words into the language. Do you know (and approve of) all those below?

mountain bikes	cosmetic surgery	airmiles
wheel-clamping	bottle-banks	jacuzzis
microwave ovens	cash-dispensers	phonecards
lap-top computers	smart bombs	modems
electronic tagging	flexi-time	CD roms

Foreign Words and Phrases

A great many expressions used in English come originally from other languages but most of them are now so absorbed into English that they are no longer thought of as foreign. However, some words and phrases, like those in the following exercises, have retained their original spelling, pronunciation and foreign identity.

1   FRENCH Put each of the following expressions into its correct place in the sentences below.

tête-à-tête	hors d'oeuvre	cul-de-sac	bon voyage
rendezvous	blasé	carte blanche	grand prix
nouveaux riches	chic		

(a)   The advantage of living in a _____ is that there is no through traffic, so it's very quiet.
(b)   Let's order. I'm hungry. I'm going to start with a nice _____.
(c)   The boss didn't tell me how he wanted the project carried out. He gave me _____ to do it as I thought best.
(d)   The French _____ was won by a Brazilian driver in an Italian car.
(e)   _____, and send us a post-card when you arrive!
(f)   She chooses her clothes, hair-style and make-up so that she is in the latest fashion. She always looks very _____.
(g)   I have one or two ideas I'd like to discuss with you. Could we have a little _____ one day soon?
(h)   He was very excited when his first book was published, but now, having written over 30, he's fairly _____ about it.
(i)   That restaurant is a favourite _____ for writers and artists.
(j)   A snob tends to look down on _____ as people who have money but no class or taste.

2   FRENCH Instructions as above.

| encore | début | c'est la vie | au fait | entourage |
| façade | détente | avant garde | coup | gourmet |

(a)   If we take Charles out to dinner, we must choose a good restaurant. He's a _____.
(b)   There was a successful _____ last night. The president has been arrested and the main government buildings are in the hands of the army.
(c)   Film stars don't usually travel alone. They're normally surrounded by a large _____ of agents, secretaries and other helpers.
(d)   The audience liked her songs so much that at the end they shouted, '_____', and she obliged by singing one more.
(e)   Yes, I've had some bad luck recently, but it's no use worrying about it. _____.
(f)   I hadn't visited the country for a long time and I wasn't _____ with the most recent political developments.
(g)   He's a very _____ artist. I have no idea what he's trying to express. Very few people understand his paintings.
(h)   She made her _____ as an actress in a film at the age of 14.
(i)   That building still has its old _____ as you can see, but the rest of the building behind it has been rebuilt and modernised.
(j)   At the moment there is a _____ between the two countries. Relations are much easier.

3 LATIN Instructions as above.

status quo   **ad nauseam**   **ego**   **bona fide**
per capita   **post mortem**   **curriculum vitae**   **persona non grata**
vice versa   **pro rata**

(a) Duty-free goods may be purchased only by _____ travellers. Please show your flight-ticket when buying.

(b) Applicants for this post should write enclosing a detailed _____.

(c) Rental rates for our cars are £50 a day. Longer periods will be charged _____ with no reductions, so a one-week rental will be £350.

(d) He was barred from this country in 1985 and has been _____ ever since.

(e) Everyone must do what she wants, listen to what she says, go where she decides to go. No one else is important. She really has got a big _____.

(f) Some people just want to preserve the _____ in this country, but others want change, reform, development.

(g) A great many British people spend their holidays in America, and _____.

(h) The _____ examination showed that she died of cancer.

(i) Canada has a _____ income of over $20,000.

(j) I'm afraid he's rather a boring person. He goes on and on _____ about his political views.

4 MIXED Instructions as above.

siesta	**(Spanish)**	**kindergarten**	**(German)**
macho	**(Spanish)**	**incognito**	**(Italian)**
patio	**(Spanish)**	**bravo**	**(Italian)**
blitz	**(German)**	**graffiti**	**(Italian)**
kaput	**(German)**	**kowtow**	**(Chinese)**

(a) A man who is very hard, tough and masculine is sometimes described as '_____'.

(b) At the age of three she went to a _____ just to learn to play with other children.

(c) After lunch I like to have a _____ for an hour or so.

(d) A week after the wall was repainted, it was covered with _____ again.

(e) My television's _____. I'll have to buy a new one.

(f) You performed very well. _____!

(g) He didn't want to be recognised so he changed his appearance and travelled _____.

(h) My garden was looking very overgrown and neglected so I did a real _____ on it last Saturday. I worked all day.

(i) When the Prime Minister comes, just be polite and normal. There's no need to _____ to him.

(j) No, our house hasn't got a proper garden, just a paved _____.

Homophones

A homophone is a word which has exactly the same pronunciation as another word although the spelling and meaning are different.

E.g. One – won
nose – knows
write – right
piece – peace

1   Write a homophone for each of the following words.

(a)	two	(i)	here	(q)	hole
(b)	eye	(j)	pair	(r)	sale
(c)	guest	(k)	wait	(s)	meet
(d)	waste	(l)	steel	(t)	past
(e)	male	(m)	bored	(u)	blue
(f)	way	(n)	seize	(v)	red
(g)	wear	(o)	principal	(w)	stairs
(h)	war	(p)	caught	(x)	born

2   Instructions as above.

(a)	road	(i)	sort	(q)	praise
(b)	so	(j)	pause	(r)	ceiling
(c)	rain	(k)	main	(s)	heard
(d)	sweet	(l)	pale	(t)	sent
(e)	fair	(m)	berry	(u)	sell
(f)	bold	(n)	higher	(v)	course
(g)	miner	(o)	through	(w)	find
(h)	died	(p)	morning	(x)	idle

Abbreviations

1 For each abbreviation on the left below find another on the right which has something in common with it.

(a) a.m.   Cantab.
(b) PC   BA
(c) Oxon.   PM
(d) MP   p.m.
(e) BR   CID
(f) RN   BST
(g) GMT   RAF
(h) BBC   BC
(i) AD   ITV

2 For each abbreviation on the left below there is another in the centre and another on the right which together make a group of three abbreviations which have something in common. Make as many groups of three as you can.

(a) NHS   ft   WHO
(b) oz   Rd   Ave
(c) in   GP   PhD
(d) Con.   MA   yd
(e) St   lb   st
(f) BA   mph   Lib. Dem.
(g) mpg   Lab.   cc

3 Put each of the following abbreviations in its correct place in the sentences below.

SOS	TUC	QC	VIP	UFO	IQ
VC	HIV	CND	HQ	MBE	DIY

(a) The United Nations _____ is in New York.
(b) Now then all you _____ fans. Here's an all-purpose tool to help you in a hundred ways to do those home repairs.
(c) Although he was defended by an eminent _____, he was found guilty and sent to prison for eight years.
(d) He's extremely bright. They say he has an _____ of 160.
(e) He was the only soldier in the regiment to win the _____ in the Second World War.
(f) The _____ represents the great majority of working men and women in Britain.
(g) Scientists doing research into Aids are looking for an antidote to the _____ virus.
(h) Film-stars, prime ministers and other celebrities are entertained in the special _____ lounge at the airport.
(i) The Beatles each received an honour from the Queen. It was the _____.
(j) Their _____ was picked up on the radio by two other ships and a plane. They were rescued within hours.
(k) Some people thought the object in the sky was a _____ bringing visitors from another planet but it turned out to be a small plane.
(l) _____ will support any moves to abolish or reduce nuclear weapons.

4   Some abbreviations, like the following, are pronounced as one word.
Put each one in its correct place in the sentences below.

UNESCO   **VAT**   **NASA**
AIDS   **NATO**   **OPEC**

(a)   The price is £87 but it's subject to _____ so that will be £95.70.
(b)   _____ has been described as possibly the most deadly epidemic in the history
of the world.
(c)   _____ has announced that the next space shuttle launch will take place in
August.
(d)   The _____ nations are to meet in Geneva to decide whether to increase the
price of oil.
(e)   _____ military exercises involving American forces will be held in Britain and
Germany this winter.
(f)   An expert from _____ produced a report on primary education in
underdeveloped countries.

Similes

1   Put the following words into the correct spaces in the sentences below.

kitten   **hills**   **sheet**   **new pin**
feather   **knife**   **dust**   **flash**

(a)   I've heard that story a hundred times before. It's as old as the _____.
(b)   Her children are always beautifully dressed and as clean as a _____.
(c)   I'm afraid I find ancient history as dry as _____.
(d)   What's wrong? Are you ill? You're as white as a _____.
(e)   She went on a diet, lost several kilos and now she's as light as a _____.
(f)   The schoolchildren were very bright. They answered my questions as quick as a
_____.
(g)   After the operation I felt as weak as a _____.
(h)   He's very intelligent and quick-thinking. He's as sharp as a _____.

2   Put the correct adjectives from the following list into the sentences
below.

cool   **sober**   **good**   **poor**
thin   **deaf**   **drunk**   **fit**

(a)   He was as _____ as a lord.
(b)   I was as _____ as a judge.
(c)   He's as _____ as a church mouse.
(d)   She remained as _____ as a cucumber.
(e)   The children were as _____ as gold.
(f)   He's as _____ as a rake.
(g)   I'm as _____ as a fiddle.
(h)   He's as _____ as a post.

Proverbs

1   Match each of the following common proverbs with the most appropriate situation from the list below.

(a)   Actions speak louder than words.
(b)   Don't look a gift horse in the mouth.
(c)   When in Rome, do as the Romans.
(d)   Don't count your chickens before they're hatched.
(e)   Prevention is better than cure.

1)   Yes, you'll probably pass the exam, but don't depend on it till you hear the result.
2)   Well, the cassette recorder he gave you may have a few defects, but you shouldn't complain. It cost you nothing.
3)   I'm not impressed by fine speeches. Why doesn't the government *do* something?
4)   Don't wait till you've got flu. Try not to catch it.
5)   If you're in a foreign country, you should get used to the customs there.

2   Instructions as above.

(a)   Nothing venture, nothing gain.
(b)   Once bitten, twice shy.
(c)   A bad workman blames his tools.
(d)   Too many cooks spoil the broth.
(e)   Pride comes before a fall.

1)   I'm not investing my money in that company again. I lost everything last time I did.
2)   Ask her out to dinner. If you don't, you'll never know if she likes you.
3)   He was over-confident. He thought he couldn't go wrong, but then he got complacent and failed the all-important exam.
4)   Do we really need so many of us to do this job? Won't we get in each other's way?
5)   It's not my fault I haven't finished this typing yet. It's not a very good machine and the stuff I have to copy is very difficult to read.

SEX EQUALITY AND THE ENGLISH LANGUAGE

The increasing demand for sex equality has had an effect on English grammar and vocabulary. We used to say, of a mixed class, 'Every student must make sure *he* has *his* student card'. Many people didn't accept this. It is rather a mouthful to say 'he or she', 'his or her' all the time, so we use 'they', 'their': 'Every student must make sure *they* have *their* student card.'

The title, 'Ms', for both married and unmarried women means that they, like men, need not advertise their marital status. Some people, in fact, are so determined to avoid male dominance in language that they use adapted words like 'personkind', 'herstory' and 'wimmin'.

Actresses now call themselves 'actors'. Words like 'salesman' and 'chairman' are disappearing, to be replaced by 'salesperson', 'chairperson' or simply 'chair'.

Euphemisms

To avoid referring too directly to unpleasant, embarrassing or personal matters we often prefer to use more indirect words or phrases, which are called euphemisms.

1   Rewrite the following sentences, replacing the euphemisms, in italics, with more simple, direct words or phrases.

(a)   I'm afraid Mrs Wild *passed away* last night.
(b)   Excuse me, where's the nearest *public convenience*?
(c)   *Senior citizens* are entitled to free bus travel.
(d)   Sadly, my grandmother is *no longer with us.*
(e)   In the middle of the exam I had to *answer a call of nature.*
(f)   His hat *had seen better days.*
(g)   We had to have our dog *put to sleep.*

The following sentences are very direct. Rewrite them, replacing the parts in italics with euphemisms.

E.g. She's *very old.*
     She's not as young as she was/getting on/advanced in years.

(a)   He's *fat and ugly*.
(b)   I'm going to *vomit*.
(c)   She's a *terrible cook*.
(d)   You were *drunk* last night.
(e)   This work *is very careless*.
(f)   Grandpa *can hardly walk*.

2   Instructions as in the first exercise above.

(a)   We were obliged to *dispense with Miss Farr's services* last month.
(b)   He has been asked to leave the country due to his involvement with *activities incompatible with his diplomatic duties* here.
(c)   The state has an obligation to assist the *less privileged members of the community.*
(d)   The estate agent says the house *needs some attention.*
(e)   The ambassador said the talks were likely to *have a negative outcome.*
(f)   Tourists are advised to avoid the *less salubrious* parts of the city.
(g)   Mr West *has shown insufficient effort in the execution of his duties.*

Instructions as in the second exercise above.

(a)   Your representative *lied* to us.
(b)   The talks were a *waste of time*.
(c)   He's *always late for work*.
(d)   Your product is *very badly-made*.
(e)   Our relations with your country *are awful*.
(f)   It would be *stupid to go on strike* now.
(g)   *You owe us money.*
(h)   We were *very angry* with your letter.

Britain

The election system

Put the following words or phrases in its correct place in the passage below.

proportional representation	polling day	by-election
Member of Parliament	canvassing	eligible
call an election	secret ballot	deposit
House of Commons	constituents	campaigns
stand for election	constituencies	turn-out
General Election	polling stations	

Middleford. Election Result.	Mr G. Smith (Labour)	30,000 votes
No. of registered voters: 100,000	Mrs R. Green (Conservative)	25,000 votes
	Mrs L. Jones (Independent)	10,000 votes
	Mr W. Woods (Communist)	5,000 votes

A (a) _____ has just taken place all over the United Kingdom. These must take place every five years unless the Prime Minister decides to (b) _____ earlier. Above is the result in Middleford, one of the approximately 635 (c) _____ into which the country is divided for this purpose. (d) _____ was last Thursday, when the election (e) _____ and door-to-door (f) _____ stopped and the people of Middleford went to the (g) _____ to make their choice, in a (h) _____, from the four candidates (anyone over the age of 21 can (i) _____, on payment of a (j) _____ of £500, which is returned if he or she receives at least 5% of the votes cast). Voting is not compulsory and the number of people (k) _____ to vote in Middleford (everyone over 18) was 100,000, so the (l) _____ was 70%. Now Mr Smith will become the (m) _____ for Middleford, which means he will represent the people of Middleford in the (n) _____ in London. If he should die or be forced to give up his seat, the people of Middleford will have to vote again, in a (o) _____ to replace him. It is a very simple system and Mr Smith will try to represent all his (p) _____ fairly, whether they voted for him or not. However, the fact remains that most voters in Middleford voted for candidates (and parties) other than Mr Smith, and their votes are now lost. It is seats which are important in Parliament, not votes, and it is easy to see why the smaller parties would like a system of (q) _____, in which the number of votes they won was reflected in the number of seats they received in Parliament.

The House of Commons

1   Put each of the following words or phrases in its correct place in the passage below.

Cabinet	benches	Foreign Secretary
backbenchers	Budget	Shadow Cabinet
Prime Minister	Speaker	Home Secretary
ministers	front bench	Leader of the Opposition
debates	Opposition	Chancellor of the Exchequer

This is the House of Commons, where Members of Parliament take their seats on the green leather (a) _____ according to their party and position. One of them is chosen to be the (b) _____, who acts as a kind of chairperson of the (c) _____ which take place in the House. In front of and on the right of this person sit the MPs of the biggest party, which forms the government, and facing them sit the MPs of the parties who oppose them, the (d) _____. The leaders of these two groups sit at the front on each side. MPs without special positions in their parties sit behind their leaders at the back. They are called (e) _____. The leader of the government, the (f) _____, sits on the government (g) _____, of course, next to his or her (h) _____. The most important of these form the (i) _____. The minister responsible for relations with other countries is called the (j) _____. The one responsible for law and security is called the (k) _____. The one who deals with financial matters and prepares the annual (l) _____ speech on the economic state of the country is called the (m) _____. Opposite this group sits the (n) _____ (the main person in the largest party opposing the government) and the (o) _____, each member of which specialises in a particular area of government.

2   The picture below shows a view of the House of Commons from the Public Gallery. After completing the exercise above, match each of the following people or groups of people with a letter on the picture.

backbenchers	Government	Leader of the Opposition
Cabinet	Prime Minister	Shadow Cabinet
Opposition	Speaker	

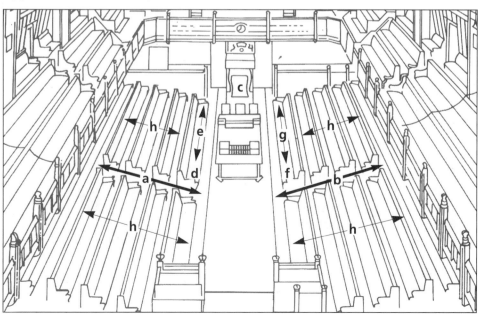

Famous places

The following places in London are associated with certain important institutions and are often used in the media and in general conversation to refer to those institutions. Put each one in its correct place in the sentences below.

Whitehall	**Fleet Street**	**Scotland Yard**	**Buckingham Palace**
the City	**10 Downing Street**	**the West End**	**the Old Bailey**
Westminster			

(a)   His criminal career started with theft and pick-pocketing and ended up at _____ on a murder charge.

(b)   Although he's only just entered Parliament, he's already aiming at _____.

(c)   There are likely to be late nights and angry arguments at _____ when the new tax proposals are debated next week.

(d)   _____ has denied reports that the Queen is shortly going to abdicate.

(e)   After the prison escape, _____ alerted all police forces to be on the look-out for the man.

(f)   He's an important man in _____. He's director of a big bank or insurance firm or something.

(g)   She's a good actress but she won't really feel she's succeeded until she has a leading part in _____.

(h)   There are rumours in _____ about the possible launching of a new newspaper next year.

(i)   There have been growing complaints that bureaucracy in _____ is slowing down the enforcement of government legislation.

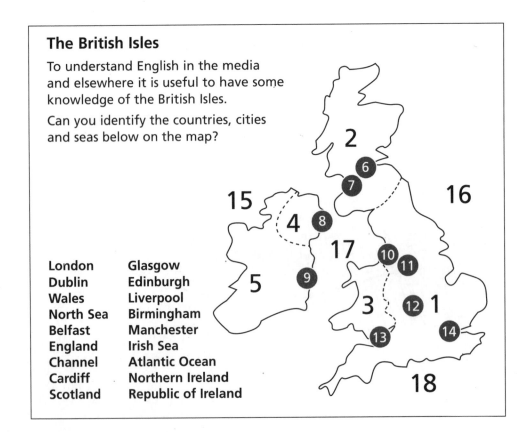

The British Isles

To understand English in the media and elsewhere it is useful to have some knowledge of the British Isles.

Can you identify the countries, cities and seas below on the map?

London	Glasgow
Dublin	Edinburgh
Wales	Liverpool
North Sea	Birmingham
Belfast	Manchester
England	Irish Sea
Channel	Atlantic Ocean
Cardiff	Northern Ireland
Scotland	Republic of Ireland

Word Games

1   Write sentences using only one vowel.

    e.g. Alan's grandma always had asthma attacks.
          Ellen's seven nephews were seen everywhere.
          John's got to go to Oxford tomorrow.

2   Rearrange the nonsense compound nouns in each group below so that they make eight real compound nouns.

DOG	JET	FAN	LAG
FOLK	TREE	FIRE	WAVE
JUMBO	ORGAN	BRAIN	TABLE
FLOWER	LIFTER	BEAUTY	ARREST
FAMILY	COLLAR	COFFEE	ESCAPE
MOUTH	STICK	HOUSE	QUEEN
SHOP	SONG	NEST	MAIL
LIP	BED	JET	EGG

3   Write sentences in which each word begins with the same letter.
    e.g. Eva eyed Eric's eclairs enviously.
          Sally says she saw someone steal six silver spoons.
          The three Turkish tourists took the two-twenty train.

4   Complete the words below by putting in the missing double letters,
    e.g. O—RE— (to keep down) OPPRESS
        CO— — (beverage)   COFFEE

      SE — —   CO — I — —
      PO — E —   MI —I — I — I
      GO — E —   MA — RE —
      A — A — IN   SU — E — E —
      E — AY   TA — —
      CA — E — E   K — — E —

5   'Ough' is pronounced quite differently in 'bough' and 'enough'. How many other pronunciations of 'ough' can you find? Altogether there are at least 8.

6   Rearrange the letters of each nonsense word below to form a real word which has a similar meaning to the word in brackets.

e.g. (strange) launuus
    Answer: unusual

a) (funny)	gainsum ·	claimco	omushuro	rashiliou
b) (child)	houty	greenate	grenytous	cotenadles
c) (think)	sume	endrop	droncise	lampettonce

Key

The answer to some of the exercises in this book are a matter of opinion. In these case, no answer is given here.

Dictionary Practice

Pronunciation (p.1)

1 a) swear, switch, b) quay, see, c) colonel, third, d) company, flood, e) timber, number, f) yacht, hot, g) rise, advise, h) theatre, think, i) aisle, sigh, j) coat, low **2** a) gone, shone, b) worry, hurry, c) comb, dome, d) owe, go, e) four, door, f) show, though, g) tough, stuff, h) word, third, i) lose, choose, j) prize, rise

Stress and Spelling (p.1)

(Check answers in your dictionary)

Meaning (p.2)

1 a) the joint b) the tree c) the garden d) a school e) the ordeal **2** bowler, busby, helmet, beret, cap; hull, deck, bridge, porthole, funnel; brakes, boot, bumpers, dashboard, windscreen; balance, statement, overdraft, account, deposit; crawl, stroll, stagger, limp, creep **3** a) dimwit - all the others mean 'friend', b) sluggish - all the others mean 'fast', c) adore - all the others mean 'hate', d) nadir - all the others mean 'the top', e) parched - all the others mean 'wet', f) grant - all the others mean 'beg'

Word Parts (p.3)

1 geese, oxen, salmon, aircraft, mice, halves, oases, diagnoses **2** a) quarrelsome b) mountaineers c) triangular d) informative **3** fire-brigade, fire-prooof, fire-arm, lighthouse, light-hearted, light-fingered, playpen, playboy, playwright

Word Use (p.3)

1 a) from b) in, into, c) in d) at, by, with **2** a) I leant my bike against the wall. b) She walked the dog in the park. c) He drives his taxi very carefully. d) No object possible. e) She sat the baby on the chair. f) No object possible. g) He marched his men up the hill. h) No object possible.

Topics

City Life (p.4)

a) city-dwellers b) irresistible lure c) metropolis d) cosmopolitan e) stimulation f) anonymity g) cost of living h) pollution i) urban j) to breed crime k) commuter l) congestion

Issues in Education (p.4)

a) classless b) streaming c) gifted d) potential e) elite f) privileged g) labelled h) inferiority complex i) divisive j) conventional k) spontaneity l) cram

Fashion in Clothes (p.5)

a) individualists b) slaves to fashion c) haute couture d) fashion houses e) trends f) trendy g) dictate h) the latest fashion i) personal ornaments j) slavishly k) dictates l) conformists

The Environment (p.5)

a) ecological b) sewage c) extinction d) deforestation e) acid rain f) pesticides g) herbicides h) organic i) disposal j) animal rights k) sustainable l) enlightened

Advertising (p.6)

a) implicit b) subtle c) exploit d) ubiquitous e) catchy jingles f) bombard g) brainwash
h) beneficial i) informative j) watchdog k) blatant l) misleading

How Much Freedom Should Children Have? (p.6)

a) permissive b) adolescence c) formative d) run wild e) juvenile delinquency f) authoritarian
g) possessive h) rebelliousness i) suppress j) upbringing k) inhibited

Censorship (p.7)

a) excessive b) gratuitous c) corrupting d) masquerading e) unscrupulous f) perverted
g) degrades h) banned i) counter-productive j) infringes k) moral standards l) safeguards

Love (p.7)

a) idolise b) hero-worship c) mature d) infatuation e) flirtation f) partners g) one-sided
h) mutual i) platonic j) stable k) compatible l) complement

Attitudes to Work and Leisure (p.8)

a) aspire b) initiative c) constructively d) aimless e) fulfilment f) conditioned g) regimentation
h) rewarding i) creativity j) 9 to 5 k) scope l) challenge

The Purpose of State Punishment (p.8)

a) reform b) rehabilitate c) deterrent d) retribution e) wrongdoer f) misdeeds g) crime doesn't
pay h) corporal punishment i) death penalty j) barbaric k) humane l) law-abiding

Related Word Groups

Body (p.9)

a) jaw, lid, lash, pupil, temple, lobe, gums, nostril b) elbow, biceps, forearm, thumb, palm,
wrist, fist, knuckles c) calf, thigh, shin, instep, heel, sole, toes, ankle

Books (p.9)

1 a) manuscript b) proofs c) volume d) publication e) copy f) hardback, paperback g) bestseller h) edition i) thriller j) whodunnit 2 a) An encyclopaedia is usually in several volumes,
while a dictionary is normally only one, b) A whodunnit (= who did it? i.e. Who was the
murderer?) c) A thriller, because it is thrilling, exciting. d) From a government or similar
publication. e) 'Have you got a copy of …?' f) The author must hand in the manuscript.
g) The proofs must be checked. h) Every author hopes for a bestseller i) Buy paperbacks
instead of hardbacks. 3 a) browse b) skip c) look up d) refer to e) read from cover to cover, dip
into f) wade through g) peruse h) skim i) flip through 5 a) key b) acknowledgements c) 'blurb'
d) glossary e) index f) dedication g) footnotes, appendix h) bibliography i) frontispiece
j) contents k) chronology

Dirt and Damage (p.11)

1 a) scratched b) faded c) shabby d) torn e) soiled f) smeared g) rusty h) stained i) shop-soiled
j) smudged k) blunt l) filthy

Drinking (p.12)

1 a) never drinks alcohol b) doesn't want other people to know he drinks c) only drinks with
other people, e.g. at parties d) has a drink from time to time e) is addicted to alcohol
f) is often drunk g) is a poor person, often homeless, who drinks anything, anywhere h) drinks
a lot i) runs a pub j) serves people in a pub k) produces beer in large quantities 3 a) a non-
alcoholic fruit drink b) a mixed alcoholic drink c) a last (alcoholic) drink before going to bed
d) a last drink before driving e) a mixture of beer and lemonade (or a similar drink)
f) a mixture of wine or spirits and hot water, sugar, lemon etc. g) a refreshing non-alcoholic
drink, e.g. squash, Coca-Cola h) a single drink of spirits 5 a) corkscrew b) pub crawl, hangover
c) vineyard d) toast e) sip f) cheers g) breathalyzer h) drop i) booze j) intoxicated k) stagger

7 a) 'sober' means 'not drunk'. b) 'tipsy' means 'slightly drunk' c) 'fizzy' means 'effervescent' (with bubbles), 'still' means 'not fizzy' (especially soft drinks) d) 'draught beer' is served direct from the barrel or container, not in bottles e) you are a 'teetotal' if you never drink alcohol but if you are' on the wagon', you might only have stopped temporarily f) 'vintage wine' is a good wine of a certain age and maturity, 'plonk' is colloquial for cheap, ordinary wine g) you can drink in a 'pub', but an 'off-licence' is a shop selling alcohol to take away h) whisky is 'neat' when nothing else is added to the glass, 'on the rocks' means 'with ice' i) 'Dutch courage' is the confidence you get from a drink, e.g. whisky, but 'to go Dutch' means that each person pays for him or herself, e.g. in a pub

Driving (p.13)

1 a) indicated b) accelerated c) overtook d) turned on e) dipped f) sounded g) swerved h) applied i) skidded j) reversed k) pulled up l) checked m) fastened n) adjusted o) started p) released

Food (p.14)

1 a) peck at b) chew, swallow c) consume d) polish off e) gorge f) gnaw g) bolt, digest h) lick **3** a) pig b) cow c) pig d) deer e) calf f) sheep g) pig **4** a) a chicken b) a nut c) cheese d) dough e) an orange f) a rabbit g) a loaf h) a joint of meat **5** a) meat b) a hard-boiled egg c) a pancake d) cream e) a chicken f) potatoes g) eggs h) a cake **6** a) 'starving' means 'very hungry', 'parched' means 'very dry', 'very thirsty' b) a 'snack' is a very quick, light meal but 'a square meal' is a proper, substantial meal c) bread goes 'stale' after a few days and goes 'mouldy' after a few more days when a fungus begins to grow on it d) 'peckish' means 'rather hungry' but 'ravenous' means 'extremely hungry', 'starving' e) unattractive or badly-cooked food is 'uneatable', but food which is simply not suitable or possible for humans to eat is 'inedible' f) a 'beer-bottle' is a bottle intended to contain beer, possibly empty, but a 'bottle of beer' is a bottle with beer in it g) a 'starter' is a small dish before the main course of a meal, a 'dessert' (fruit, pudding) comes at the end h) a 'restaurant' serves complete lunches and dinners only, but a 'cafe' serves all meals and often simple snacks and drinks

Friends (p.16)

1 a) compatriot b) pen-pal c) companion d) partner e) mate f) bosom pal g) rival h) companion i) old flame j) mate k) foe l) colleague m) fair-weather friend n) confidant o) mate p) acquaintance q) associate

Adjectives from Famous People (p.16)

Churchillian, Machiavellian, Napoleonic, Maoist, Elizabethan, Stalinist, Hitlerite, Confucian, Leninist, Kafkaesque, Thatcherite, Freudian, Ritzy, Marxist, Platonic

Light (p.17)

1 a) floodlight b) flare c) glow d) flash, lightning e) twinkle f) dazzle g) flicker h) spark i) sparkle **2** a) headlights b) traffic-lights c) torch d) son et lumière e) limelight f) footlights g) spotlight h) searchlight i) chandelier j) lantern

Materials (p.18)

1 a) comfortable soft trousers b) a ship's sail etc. c) jeans d) a woman's expensive, warm coat e) bathroom windows f) church windows g) the roof of a shed or cheap hut h) a man's old-fashioned light summer hat i) a wall j) cutlery **2** a) a wine-bottle stopper b) a woman's expensive evening dress c) shoes, a casual jacket d) fine bed-sheets e) an ordinary soldier's uniform f) packing material g) a man's hard-wearing sports-jacket h) fine cups etc. i) old ships j) a lawn

American English 1 (p.18)

shop, tap, postman, sweets, flat, town centre, drawing pin, petrol, pavement, 1st year university student, rubbish, lift, boot, bonnet, cinema, queue

Money (p.19)

1 a) currency b) counterfeit c) numismatist d) counterfoil, expenditure e) bounce f) standing order g) statement h) legal tender **2** a) broke b) make ends meet c) chickenfeed d) quid e) mortgage f) I.O.U. g) hire purchase, instalments

Typing practice (p.19)

Each sentence uses all the letters of the alphabet.

Numbers (p.20)

a) scores b) cardinal, ordinal c) dozen d) gross e) Roman f) even, odd g) digits h) odd, i) good j) average k) round

People (p.20)

1 a) a day-dreamer b) a busybody c) a dare-devil d) a rolling stone e) a sponger f) a battle-axe g) a golden boy h) a slow coach i) a crank j) a pain in the neck k) a lone wolf l) a tomboy **2** a) a wind-bag b) a miser c) a name-dropper d) a slave-driver e) a jay-walker f) a layabout g) a litter-lout h) a road-hog i) a clock-watcher j) a fare dodger k) a slob l) a tear-away

Small Quantities (p.21)

1 a) speck b) crumb c) blade d) dot e) grain f) shred g) fragment h) glimmer i) grain j) trace k) trace **2** a) drop b) clue c) breath d) drop e) dash f) hint g) scrap h) puff i) scrap j) item k) flake

Social Types (p.22)

1 a) life and soul of the party b) wet blanket c) good mixer d) gate-crasher e) wallflower f) chatterbox g) gossip h) femme fatale i) Don Juan j) social climber **3** a) good company b) snob c) killjoy d) early bird e) loner f) bore g) jet-setter h) parasite i) socialite j) trouble-maker

Sounds (p.23)

1 a) scream b) moan c) cheer d) boo e) chant f) gasp g) snort h) drone i) whimper j) yell **3** a) toll b) chime c) tinkle d) thud e) sizzle f) blare g) hiss h) swish i) clink j) pop **5** a) squelch b) plop c) rattle d) boom e) chirrup f) squeak g) rumble h) click i) hoot j) murmur **7** a) large bell b) clock c) violin-string breaking d) iron gates closing e) car horn f) electronic personal caller g) gun h) light rain on window i) wood fire burning j) car braking at speed k) horses' hoofs on road l) bath-water going down plug-hole m) spoon tapping empty glass

Space Travel (p.25)

a) gravity b) manned c) astronaut d) launching pad e) launch f) countdown g) lift-off h) splashdown i) spacecraft j) orbit k) dock l) mission

Sport (p.26)

1 a) a pitch b) a pool c) a course d) a track e) a court f) a court g) a court h) a ring i) a range j) a rink k) a circuit l) a track/course **2** a) puck-stick b) bow/arrows c) club/tee d) racket/net e) racket/shuttlecock f) gloves/gumshield g) helmet/steering-wheel h) whip/reins i) saddle/ handlebars j) rifle/target k) toboggan/goggles l) parallel bars/mat m) épée/mask **3** a) horse-racing ('The race has begun!') b) boxing ('Assistants out of the ring!') c) golf ('Get out of the way of the ball!') d) football ('Referee, someone's broken the rules!') e) tennis, table-tennis ('The score is forty points to zero.') f) athletics ('Get ready to start the race.') g) football etc. ('The score is three goals to zero.') h) archery, shooting ('Right in the middle of the target!') i) show-jumping ('The rider has lost four penalty points.')

Time (p.27)

1 a) the small hours b) digital c) local time d) time zones e) chronological f) decade, century g) spell h) era i) turn of the century **2** a) Dawn is the first light of day and dusk is the last b) a month can be any period of 28 days, but a calendar month specifies that one of the 12 named months of the year, e.g. April, is meant c) a leap year is one in which February has 29 days

Tools and Equipment (p.27)

1 a) a stethoscope b) a rake c) a whip d) a rolling pin e) a hose f) an axe g) a baton h) an anvil i) a plane j) an exposure meter k) a spanner l) an anchor **2** a) a bow b) a bucket c) a net d) a tape measure e) a scalpel f) a torch g) a truncheon h) a trowel i) a drier j) a spade k) a pneumatic drill l) a compass **3** a) a turntable b) flippers c) a briefcase d) a catalogue e) a vacuum cleaner f) radar g) scaffolding h) a parking meter i) a hearse j) blueprints k) a palette l) a crane **4** a) a score b) a sniffer dog c) a loom d) a whistle e) a last f) headphones g) a plough h) a kiln i) a filing cabinet j) a clapperboard k) a drill l) a till

Word Formation

Word Forms (p.29)

1 a) beautiful b) beautician c) beautify **2** a) payment b) payable c) payee **3** a) receptionist b) receipt c) receptive **4** a) heroism b) heroically c) heroine **5** a) production b) producers c) unproductive **6** a) explanatory b) inexplicable c) explanation **7** a) incomparably, comparison b) comparative **8** a) inadvisable b) advisory c) advisability **9** a) admirers b) admiration c) admirable **10** a) stabilise b) instability c) unstable **11** a) economise b) uneconomical c) economic **12** a) residence b) residential c) residents **13** a) comforting b) uncomfortable c) discomfort **14** a) deaths b) deadly c) deaden **15** a) demonstrators b) undemonstrative c) demonstrably **16** a) imitation b) imitative c) inimitable **17** a) argument b) argumentative c) arguably **18** a) unrepeatable b) repetitive c) repetition **19** a) unfailingly b) failure c) failing **20** a) discourage b) courageously c) encouragement **21** a) unrealistic b) reality c) realist **22** a) falsifying b) falsehood c) falsity **23** a) prophet, prophecy b) prophetic **24** a) indescribable b) descriptive c) description **25** a) friendship b) befriended c) unfriendly **26** a) sensation b) insensitive c) senseless **27** a) fame b) infamous, infamy **28** a) defensive b) indefensible c) defence **29** a) disagreeable b) agreement c) agreeable **30** a) possessions b) possessive c) possessor **31** a) differ b) differentiate c) differences **32** a) activists b) activated c)inactive **33** a) formative b) deformity c) formation **34** a) compulsory b) compulsion c) compelling **35** a) creator b) creative c) creation **36** a) enthusiastically b) enthusiast c) enthuse **37** a) necessitate b) necessarily c) necessities **38** a) indestructible b) destruction c) destructive **39** a) management b) unmanageable c) managerial/management **40** a) unbelievable b) beliefs c) disbelief

Portmanteau Words (p.33)

Swatch: Swiss + watch, hazchem: hazardous + chemicals, Chunnel: Channel + tunnel, vegeburger: vegetarian + (ham)burger, fantabulous: fantastic + fabulous, brunch: breakfast + lunch, Oxbridge: Oxford + Cambridge, camcorder: camera + video recorder, shopaholic: shopping + alcoholic, ginormous: gigantic + enormous, motel: motor + hotel, Interpol: international + police, guesstimate: guess + estimate, ScotRail: Scotland + railway, Amex: American + express, Oxfam: Oxford + famine, Eurovision: Europe + television, fanzine: fan-club + magazine, ecotastrophe: ecological + catastrophe, docudrama: documentary + drama

Prefixes (p.34)

1 a) pseudo b) out c) arch d) mal e) arch f) out g) mal h) pseudo i) mal j) out **2** a) name under which an author writes instead of his or her real name b) fiercest rivals c) bad, inefficient administration d) extra-large sized clothes e) poor, insufficient nutrition f) falsely pretending to be religious g) a principal, especially bad villain h) to stay longer than your host wishes you to stay **3** a) neo b) fore c) a d) hyper e) neo f) hyper g) a h) fore i) fore j) hyper **4** a) a modern form of imperialism b) a person who believes there is no God c) an indication of what is to happen in the future d) an extremely large supermarket e) very high blood pressure f) a conclusion which was known or expected before g) not symmetric, irregular h) someone who believes in the old Fascist ideas **5** uniform, decade, century, quadrangle, monocle, tricycle, bicycle, bipeds, quadrupeds, binoculars, tripod, octopus, monorail, sextet, quintet, quartet, trio, bigamy, bilingual, pentathlon, septuagenarian, duologue, monologues, nonagenarian, centenarian, octogenarian, triplets **6** a) 200th anniversary or an event b) five-sided figure c) 100th anniversary of an event d) flag with three coloured stripes e) uninteresting, without change f) athletics contest in which each competitor takes part in ten events g) someone between 59 and 70 years old h) five children from one birth i) cut or divide into two parts j) one hundredth of a dollar k) aircraft with two pairs of wings l) parliament with two chambers m) cycle designed with one wheel n) four children from one birth o) mythical animal with one horn

Suffixes (p.36)

1 a) cide b) phobia c) gamy d) phobia e) cide f) gamy g) phobia h) cide **2** a) a solution or powder which kills germs b) fear or hatred of foreigners c) killing one's own father d) a society where it is the custom for a person to have a single wife or husband e) killing one's own brother f) fear of open spaces **3** a) monger b) phile c) monger d) maniac e) phile f) monger g) maniac h) maniac **4** a) someone obsessed with setting fire to property b) a love of France and French culture c) someone who loves England and English culture d) an obsession e) someone who sells fish from a shop f) someone who is obsessed with films **5** a) like b) most c) worthy d) like e) like f) worthy g) most h) worthy **6** a) a practical, efficient manner b) his main thought, the one at the very front of his mind c) a car that is fit for use on the road d) a comment worth making a note of and remembering e) a statue which looks almost alive f) the defences furthest out from the centre **7** a) some b) wards c) esque d) wards e) some f) wards g) some h) esque **8** a) boys who are always quarrelling b) apparently confident c) a figure as striking and impressive as a statue d) a movement towards the ground e) a person who makes you tired and irritated f) a novel in the style of the writer, Kafka **9** a) scope b) let c) scape d) ling e) ette f) scape g) let h) scope i) scape **10** a) an insect so small it can only be seen properly through a microscope b) a small, young pig c) a small, young duck d) a small kitchen e) a marvellous cloud formation f) a small book **11** a) is interested in birds b) is interested in stamps c) believes in equal rights for women d) is interested in coins e) gives large amounts of money to charity f) performs post-mortems on dead bodies g) speaks many languages h) writes plays i) is an expert on earthquakes j) looks after people's hands and fingernails k) makes up medicines l) studies the weather m) sets fire to property n) stuffs dead animals o) hates women p) walks in his or her sleep q) is an expert on China r) looks after people's feet s) is a handwriting expert.

Compound Adjectives (p.38)

1 a) That's a dangerous-looking thing. b) Mr Reed is a London-born accountant. c) She is always very smartly-dressed. d) It was painted a brick-red colour. e) She had cat-like eyes. f) It was a happy-sad occasion. g) The tower is mushroom-shaped. h) He was world-famous. i) We had to write a 200-word composition. **2** a) It was an awful-tasting meal. b) Only single-engine/single-engined planes can land here. c) A five-storey building suddenly collapsed. d) We walked along a red-carpeted corridor. e) This machine is hand-operated. f) The new director is an Oxford-educated economist. g) He is very broad-shouldered. h) She's always very self-satisfied. i) My sister is very dress-conscious. **3** a) We'll have a French-speaking guide. b) The walls were sky-blue. c) I looked at the sea, which was blue-green. d) The ship sailed with an eight-man crew. e) She was fair-haired. f) The new, American-built, machinery will arrive next month. g) I heard a strange-sounding voice. h) These are man-eating tigers. i) He is always bad-tempered. **4** a) The experiment was done with gas-filled balloons. b) My teenage son is football-mad. c) I'm afraid my wife is very free-spending. d) He is certainly well-intentioned. e) They are very bad-mannered. f) The firm is New York-based. g) Those cars are very high-priced. h) The noise was ear-splitting! i) I need a four-door car.

Noun Plurals (p.39)

1 a) mice, geese, feet b) companies, stories, delays, keys c) chiefs, thieves, roofs, knives, safes d) photos, studios, Echoes, heroes e) passers-by, commanders-in-chief, brief-cases, police-cars, courts-martial/court-martials f) sheep, deer, aircraft **2** a) crises b) chateaux c) memoranda d) analyses e) bureaux f) strata g) theses h) phenomena i) criteria j) media

Problem Words

Confusing Word Pairs (p.40)

1 a) disused b) misused c) misused d) disused **2** a) illegible b) unreadable c) illegible d) unreadable **3** a) dependent b) dependant c) dependant d) dependent **4** a) historical b) historic c) historical d) historic **5** a) immigration b) emigration **6** a) unsatisfied b) dissatisfied c) dissatisfied d) unsatisfied **7** a) suit b) suite c) suite d) suit **8** a) prophesy b) prophecy **9** a) devise b) device c) device d) devise **10** a) enquiries b) inquiries c) enquiries d) inquiry **11** a) exhaustive b) exhausting c) exhausting d) exhaustive **12** a) uninterested b) disinterested c) uninterested d) disinterested **13** a) counsel b) council c) counsel d) council **14** a) counsellor b) councillor **15** a) unknown b) infamous c) infamous d) unknown **16** a) Surely b) certainly c) surely d) certainly **17** a) diary b) dairy c) dairy d) Diary **18** a) complement b) compliment c) compliment d) complement **19** a) First b) at first c) At first d) First **20** a) at last b) lastly c) At last d) lastly

Eponymous Words (p.43)

Captain Boycott was a landlord's agent who made himself unpopular in the 1880s struggle between the Irish peasants and their absent landlords. The peasants refused to pay him any rent and he was shunned by the whole community. **Louis Braille** was a blind Frenchman who invented a system of reading and writing for the blind. **Joseph Ignace Guillotin** (1738 - 1814) was a French physician who advocated the use of the guillotine in 1789. **Charles Macintosh** (1760 - 1843) invented the Macintosh, a waterproof coat made of rubberised cloth. **Vidkun Quisling** was a Norwegian officer and diplomat who betrayed his country by preparing the way for invasion by the Germans. He was executed after the liberation in 1945, but his name lives on as the generic word for a traitor. **Mikhail Kalashnikov** was the inventor of the Russian sub-machine-gun, used especially by terrorists and guerrillas. **Etienne de Silhouette** (1709 - 67) was the Finance Minister to Louis XV of France. He was well-known for policies of cheapness and economy, thus his name was given to the cheap and economical cut-out portraits popular at the time. **James Watt** (1736 - 1819) was a Scottish engineer who improved and patented the steam engine in 1769. The **Marquis de Sade** (1740 - 1814) was a French writer and soldier whose name has given expression to the practice of sadism. The **Earl of Cardigan** (1797 - 1868) gave his name to the knitted jacket or sweater which buttons up the front. **Lázló Biro** was a Hungarian who patented the first ball-point pen in Hungary, 1938. **Count Alessandro Volta** (1745 - 1827), an Italian physicist, gave his name to the derived SI unit of electrical potential.

Difficult Verb Pairs (p.44)

1 a) fallen b) felled c) fell **2** a) founded b) found c) founded **3** a) bounded b) bounded c) bound **4** a) saw b) sawed c) sawed **5** a) grounded b) ground c) ground **6** a) wound b) wounded c) wind **7** a) laid b) lay c) laid d) lie e) lay f) lie **8** a) born b) borne c) borne **9** a) costed b) cost c) costed **10** a) hung b) hanged c) hung **11** a) stricken b) struck c) stricken

Ambiguous Words (p.45)

a) correct/not left b) with light skin or hair/reasonable c) amusing/strange, peculiar d) without work to do/lazy e) know who he was/accept him as President f) inquisitive/strange, peculiar g) inexpensive/poor quality h) due, scheduled/obliged, had to i) physically strong/influential j) felt suspicion/ caused others to suspect him k) envious/protective l) invite to her home for dinner-party etc./amuse with jokes etc. m) probably will/ought to, has an obligation to n) ask me for help/I didn't like him o) well-liked/aimed at a wide circulation, non-intellectual p) perhaps he phoned/I'm annoyed he didn't phone q) ready/willing r) said they definitely did it/made them do and accepted no excuses s) exploited unfairly/took benefit from, put into use

False Friends (p.46)

1 a) present b) actual c) present **2** a) ignore b) not know c) ignore **3** a) wonderful b) formidable c) formidable d) wonderful **4** a) camping b) camp-site **5** a) morale b) moral c) morale d) moral **6** a) attend b) frequent c) frequent d) attend **7** a) adequate b) suitable c) suitable d) adequate **8** a) subject b) argument c) argument d) subject **9** a) possibly b) eventually c) possibly

d) eventually **10** a) dancing b) dance-hall **11** a) experience b) experiment c) experience d) experiment **12** a) fabricate b) manufacture c) fabricate d) manufacture **13** a) driver b) chauffeur c) chauffeur d) driver **14** a) attend b) assist c) attend d) assist **15** a) pass b) take c) take, pass **16** a) remark b) notice c) notice d) remark **17** a) souvenir b) memory c) souvenir d) memory **18** a) stamp b) print c) print d) stamp **19** a) meeting b) reunion c) meeting, reunion **20** a) nice b) sympathetic c) nice d) sympathetic **21** a) corpse b) Corps c) Corps d) corpse **22** a) voyage b) journey c) journey d) voyage **23** a) legend b) key c) key d) legend **24** a) obtain b) become c) become d) obtain **25** a) On the contrary b) On the other hand c) on the other hand d) On the contrary **26** a) review b) critic c) critic, review

Idiom

Alliterative Expressions (p.51)

1 a) rat race b) brickbats c) chit-chat d) ship-shape e) mish-mash f) wishy-washy **2** a) pitter-patter b) zigzag c) sob-story d) creepy-crawly e) sing-song f) Flip-flops **3** a) weight-watcher b) hot-head c) tittle-tattle d) riff-raff e) tell-tale f) topsy-turvy

Animals (p.52)

1 a) bookworm b) dog-collar c) puppy fat d) wolf in sheep's clothing e) wolf-whistles f) dog's life g) stag party h) underdog i) wild-goose chase **2** a) dog-eared b) fly on the wall c) bird's-eye view d) cat's eyes e) guinea pig f) frog in my throat g) pigeon-holes **3** a) ram b) monkey c) badgered d) hounded e) ducked f) worm g) fox h) dogged

Body (p.53)

1 a) brave, resolute b) mean, not generous c) generous d) businesslike, unemotional e) conceited, self-important f) cowardly, nervous g) with very good hearing h) silent, unwilling to speak i) hypocritical j) over-romantic k) insensitive to criticism **2** a) head b) shoulder c) elbow d) thumb e) finger f) foot g) mouth h) shin i) head j) back

Nationality Idioms (p.53)

Dutch courage: confidence gained from having alcoholic drink; Mexican wave: effect caused by spectators at sporting events standing up then sitting down progressively round stadium; Russian roulette: reckless 'game' of loading pistol with one bullet, spinning chamber and firing at one's own head; any very high-risk action

Collocations (p.54)

1 a) bone b) dirt c) dog d) stone e) brand f) wide g) stark h) pitch **2** a) razor b) fast c) crystal d) bone e) flat f) blind g) paper h) wide **3** a) bitter b) thin c) dire d) blank e) broad f) all-out g) rock h) blind

Colour (p.55)

1 a) in black and white b) to catch someone red-handed c) red tape d) to have green fingers e) a black sheep f) green with envy g) once in a blue moon h) in the red i) out of the blue **2** a) red-carpet treatment b) a white-collar job c) a green belt d) to see red e) a white lie f) blue-eyed boy g) rose-coloured spectacles h) a red herring

Fictional Characters in Everyday Language (p.56)

1 a) **James Bond** (daring intelligence agent in novels by Ian Fleming) b) **Billy Bunter** (fat schoolboy. always eating, in stories by Frank Richards) c) **Peter Pan** (boy who never grows up in play by J M Barrie) d) **Robinson Crusoe** (man who finds himself alone on a remote desert island in novel by Daniel Defoe) e) **Scrooge** (very mean character in Christmas Carol by Charles Dickens) f) **Man Friday** (all-purpose servant of Robinson Crusoe) g) **Superman** (character who can achieve miracles, from American comic strip) h) **Robin Hood** (legendary outlaw who 'robbed the rich to feed the poor') **2** a) **Jekyll and Hyde** (man with two contrasting personalities, one gentle and one murderous, in novel by R L Stevenson) b) **Sherlock Holmes** (brilliant, shrewd, private detective in novels by Conan Doyle) c) **Big Brother** (sinister dictator figure in totalitarian state in George Orwell's novel 1984) d) **Little Lord Fauntleroy** (very elegantly-dressed little boy in novel by F H Burnett) e) **Cinderella** (girl in fairy-tale who is treated as slave by her family) f) **Tarzan** (strong, muscular hero of stories of Edgar Rice Burroughs) g) **Walter Mitty** (man who constantly escaped from reality into heroic day-dreams in James Thurber's The Secret Life of Walter Mitty) h) **Rip Van Winkle** (man who slept for 20 years in story by Washington Irving)

Food (p.57)

1 a) a butter-fingers b) in a jam c) peanuts d) a vegetable e) no picnic f) the cream g) the salt of the earth h) full of beans i) sour grapes j) nuts k) cup of tea l) a piece of cake **2** a) cucumber b) beetroot c) toast d) pancake e) two peas in a pod f) hot potato g) hot cakes h) sardines i) water

Letter-Words (p.57)

1 A-bomb: atom bomb, E-mail: electronic mail, V-formation: aeroplanes flying in the shape of a V, T-shirt: a short-sleeved vest, V-neck: a shirt or vest with a Vshaped neckline, X-ray: electromagnetic radiation, U-turn: a 180% turn, T-junction: a road junction shaped like a letter T, A-line: a narrow, slim-fitting skirt

'Hand' (p.58)

1 a) offhand b) underhand c) cap in hand d) out of hand e) hand-to-mouth f) to hand **2** a) offhand b) in good hands c) empty-handed d) high-handed e) short-handed f) single-handed **3** a) to give him a free hand b) to keep his hand in c) to wash his hands of d) to have the upper hand e) to win hands down f) to have a hand in

Names (p.59)

1 a) bobby b) Jack of all trades c) peeping Tom d) smart Alec) Tom, Dick or Harry f) doubting Thomas **2** a) I don't know him from Adam b) keeping up with the Joneses c) robbing Peter to pay Paul d) before you could say Jack Robinson

Numbers (p.60)

1 a) two-edged compliment b) one-armed bandit c) one-track mind d) four-letter word e) one-man band f) catch 22 situation **2** a) the third degree b) sixth sense c) on first-name terms d) in her seventh heaven e) to play second fiddle f) third-rate g) to have second thoughts h) at the eleventh hour

American English 2 (p.60)

from, until, with, at the back of/behind, for, again, to, past, on, after

Pairs (p.61)

1 a) touch and go b) prim and proper c) song and dance d) by and large e) chop and change f) tooth and nail g) hard and fast h) length and breadth i) cloak and dagger j) pins and needles **2** a) sick and tired b) spick and span c) odds and ends d) ups and downs e) down and out f) pros and cons g) up and about h) safe and sound i) to and fro j) ins and outs

Phrasal Verbs (p.62)

1 a) see off b) take down c) try out d) bring up e) get down f) call off g) bring up h) put up **2** a) let down b) make up c) bear out d) put off e) leave out f) run down g) put forward h) rule out **3** a) pull down, put up b) give away c) turn out d) look up e) turn away f) do up g) put off **4** a) stand for b) account for c) get over d) run into e) get round f) take to g) come into h) take after **5** a) go back on b) be up to c) catch up with d) put up with e) make up for f) do away with g) be up to h) look down on **6** a) turn in b) turn up c) fall through d) break out e) look up f) go off g) break up h) come out **7** a) fall off b) come up c) go down d) break down e) fall out f) Hold on g) Drop in h) drop off

Rhyming Expressions (p.64)

1 a) big-wigs b) prime-time c) nitty-gritty d) culture-vulture e) higgledy-piggledy f) humdrum g) pell-mell h) brain-drain **2** a) walkie-talkie b) fun-run c) roly-poly d) silly-billy e) space-race f) mumbo-jumbo g) willy-nilly h) hanky-panky **3** a) meals-on-wheels b) make or break c) la-di-da d) wear and tear e) wine and dine f) moan and groan

Status (p.65)

a) would-be b) late c) The headmaster present d) ex- e) The present headmaster f) sacked
g) actual h) stop-gap i) in question j) -to-be k) so-called

Time (p.67)

1 a) At one time b) At the time c) at times d) for the time being e) on time f) in time **2** a) in his
time b) behind the times c) at the same time d) pressed for time e) before my time f) in no time
3 a) in the nick of time b) All in good time c) for old time's sake d) About time too e) time on
his hands f) time after time **4** a) take his time b) keep up with the times c) kill time d) make
time e) bide his time

Identification

Objects (p.67)

a) bicycle b) briefcase c) television set d) book e) piano f) watch g) tree h) pistol, revolver i) map

Newspaper Parts (p.68)

a) gossip column b) caption c) headline d) obituary e) horoscope f) editorial g) recipe h) auction
report i) football report j) travel and holidays k) parliamentary report l) gardening tips
m) television preview n) new car report

The Arts (p.68)

a) classical music concert b) exhibition of paintings c) novel d) dance, ballet e) play, theatrical
performance

Occupations (p.69)

a) men's tailor b) supermarket cashier c) airline pilot d) hospital nurse e) taxi-driver f) fireman
g) cinema usher

Occasions (p.70)

a) terrorist bomb explosion b) circus c) factory strike d) trial in court e) street demonstration

Description

People's Appearance (p.72)

1 a) lanky b) bowler hat c) double-breasted d) bow-tie e) cuff f) creases g) button-hole
h) tucked i) breast pocket j) formally **2** a) skinny b) grin c) patched d) slanting e) lapels f) plain
g) pigeon-toed h) casually i) bare-footed j) trainers **3** a) strongly-built b) broad c) waist d) clean-
shaven e) bare-headed f) closely-cropped g) expression h) buckle i) upright j) hips **4** a) teens
b) slender c) figure d) clasped e) wavy f) parted g) bow h) pleated i) polo-neck j) high-heeled
5 a) thirtyish b) folded c) bow-legged d) obese e) flat cap f) side-burns g) checked h) rolled up
i) baggy j) braces

Diagrams (p.73)

Plans (p.74)

a)

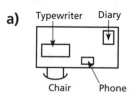

Typewriter Diary
Chair Phone

b)

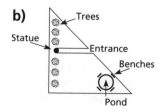

Trees
Statue
Entrance
Benches
Pond

c)

d)

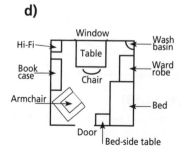

Window
Hi-Fi
Table
Wash basin
Book case
Chair
Ward robe
Armchair
Bed
Door
Bed-side table

Letter Phrases (p.75)

a) street atlas of the town b) behaviour c) doesn't pronounce the -h at the beginning of words
d) reading, (w)riting and (a)rithmetic

Maps (p.76)

a)

b)

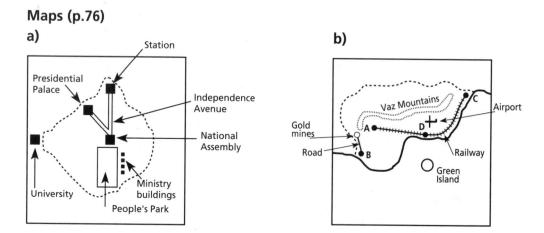

Station
Presidential Palace
Independence Avenue
National Assembly
Ministry buildings
University
People's Park

Vaz Mountains
Gold mines
Road
Airport
Railway
Green Island

Style

Newspaper Headlines (p.78)

1 a) POLLS RIGGED b) GEMS HAUL c) TWO SOUGHT d) SERVICE CHIEFS e) CABINET RESHUFFLE
2 a) GEMS b) HAUL c) RIG d) CHIEF e) SWOOP f) SEEK/SOUGHT g) GAG h) DRAMA i) POLL(S)
j) RESHUFFLE k) QUIT **4** a) FOIL b) PLEA c) BID d) HALT e) BAN f) CLASH g) BACK h) OUST
i) FLEE j) WOO k) MOVE l) QUIZ **5** a) RIDDLE b) LEAK c) ENVOY d) AXE e) LIFT f) RAP
g) BAFFLED h) CURB i) SPLIT j) PROBE k) CALL l) STORM

American English (p.79)

grey, labour, axe, plough, colour, pyjamas, aeroplane, favourite, pretence, kidnapped, centre,
dialogue, defence, theatre, catalogue, quarrelling, cheque, neighbour, signalled, traveller.

Formal English (p.81)

1 (other versions possible a) This information may be changed b) Look on the other side for
more information. c) You must keep it and show it if you're asked to. d) If you're a married
woman, write your surname when you were single. e) You must give this part of the ticket to
the usherette. f) Fill in the part at the bottom. Then tear it off. g) Stick a recent photograph of
yourself here. h) The information may be changed without warning. i) Look at the notes on the
other side. j) Put the right amount of money in. The machine doesn't give change. k) If you
don't order quickly, they may have run out of what you want. l) Trains printed in very black
letters or numbers only have sleeping cars, no ordinary carriages. m) Cross out whatever
doesn't apply to you. n) Ask inside. o) Reduced prices if you go in a group. p) You can't use it
for the underground, except for certain trains. q) Put a tick in the right box according to
whether you're married, single, divorced, widowed etc. r) You must pay a deposit when you
book, and you won't get it back. s) The date when the ticket is no good any more. t) Write the
complete name of your wife or husband. **2** (other versions possible) a) If there's anything wrong
with the machine, go back to the shop where you got it. b) Do what it says on the other side.
c) The firm doesn't take responsibility for anything which goes wrong if it isn't their fault.
d) You won't necessarily be given a place just because you've got their minimum requirements.
e) If you decide you want to keep the car longer than you originally agreed, it's important to tell
the firm immediately. f) Normally you've got to tell the bank seven days before you want to
take any money out of a Deposit Account, but if it's an emergency you can get it immediately.
g) You'll get four tickets, but if you want extra books you can get more tickets just by asking
for them. h) It's not absolutely necessary to have this letter, but if you do have it, it'll make it
much easier to get into the country. i) If you have an accident, you must pay the first £45 of
any damage caused, but if you pay an extra 95p a day, you won't have to pay anything.
3 (other versions possible) a) Any complaints should be addressed to the tour operator. b) We
regret that no refunds can be made on sale purchases. c) In the event of fire please leave in an
orderly fashion by the exits marked on the plan below. d) Travellers are advised to contact their
embassy in the event of any problems which may occur. e) Patrons are requested to refrain
from smoking. f) A Certificate of Posting may be obtained at the time of posting (to be
completed by the counter clerk) or later, on payment of a higher fee. g) Subject to alteration,
especially in adverse weather conditions. h) This receipt to be retained and produced on
request. i) Goods will not be dispatched until receipt of full remittance. j) A Certificate of
Attendance will be given on production of an Admission Slip. A note from your teacher
confirming your regular attendance is not obligatory but will greatly facilitate matters.

English in Advertising (p.83)

Trade Names 1 a) snack bar b) shoe-shop c) dry cleaners d) photo-processing shop e) photocopying firm f) women's clothes shop g) children's clothes shop h) taxi firm i) dry cleaners
j) snack bar k) garage and repair shop l) hairdressers m) travel agency n) car-hire firm
2 a) cleaning fluids b) pet food c) telephone answering machines d) beds e) rucksacks f) video
and audio home entry system **3** a) translating b) car repairs c) driving school d) security services
e) accommodation f) health and slimming studio g) travel agency h) computer services i) airline
Puns a) 'Pounds' refers first to money and second to weight. b) They go up literally but also
raise their economic and perhaps social level. c) 'Sound' refers to the quality of musical

reproduction but also means 'good', 'reliable' d) 'Sleep on it' can also mean 'think about it'
e) 'Dying for' can also mean 'wanting desperately' f) 'Snap' means 'immediate' or 'photograph'
g) 'Naturally' means 'of course' or 'in a natural way' h) 'Plane' has the same pronunciation as
'plain', meaning 'simple' i) 'Red-carpet treatment' can mean 'special service and welcome'
j) 'Sea' is pronounced like 'see' k) 'Stick using our glue' or 'remain our loyal customers'
l) Figuratively an 'Indian Summer' is a pleasant, mild autumn m) 'Food for thought' can mean
'something worth thinking about'

Spoken English

Forms of Spoken Address (p.85)

a) mum, mummy b) caller, nothing c) viewers d) grandad, grandpa e) nothing f) ladies and
gentlemen g) sir h) Your Majesty i) nothing j) darling, love, dear k) listeners l) mate m) sir
n) madam o) officer, nothing p) grandma, grannie q) dear, love r) sir s) men t) dad, daddy
u) nothing

Colloquial Responses (p.86)

1 a) My lips are sealed. b) Dump it anywhere. c) The more the merrier. d) Flattery will get you
nowhere. e) Care for a spin? 2 a) A little bird told me. b) I'm having second thoughts. c) Well,
boys will be boys. d) Beggars can't be choosers. e) Well, you can't win them all. 3 a) Let's toss
for it. b) OK. You toss. I'll call. Tails! c) I'm afraid I haven't a clue. d) Let me sleep on it. e) Oh,
it's on the tip of my tongue. 4 a) Cheers! b) Help yourself. c) No, it's my round. d) I could do
with one. e) Oh, this is on me. 5 a) Be my guest. b) Back to square one. c) Yes, by the skin of
my teeth. d) If you don't mind taking pot luck. e) Every little helps. 6 a) I'm all ears. b) I'm
keeping my fingers crossed. c) It takes all sorts. d) Well, it can't be helped. e) OK. Thanks all the
same. 7 a) You must be joking. b) Serves you right. c) Mind your own business. d) OK. Suit
yourself. e) That'll be the day. 8 a) I can't be bothered. b) Have it your own way. c) How should
I know? d) I like that! e) Rather you than me.

Exclamations (p.87)

1 a) sh! b) eh? c) giddyup! d) there, there e) boo! f) whoops! g) well? h) wow! i) whoah!
j) mm! 2 a) ta b) er c) now, now d) cheers! e) ta-ta f) hear, hear g) hi! h) oi! i) gosh!

Spoken Numbers and Measurements (p.88)

1 a) 40 - 15 + 6 = 31 b) 81 ÷ 3 = 27 c) 3 x 6 = 18 d) Queen Elizabeth I reigned from 1558 to
1603. e) ... at 7.30 p.m. on 2nd August f) ... £6.75. g) ... on 411 4850. h) ... is 44-7/509.
i) ... estimated at £2,471,850. j) The mixture is $^2/_3$ water. k) 1 litre = 1.76 pints. l) 22% of the
... m) ... was 30° C, i.e. 86° F. n) ... 4'2$^3/_4$" x 2' 8$^1/_2$". o) ... 3:0. p) ... 3:3. q) ... 30:0 to
Becker. 2 a) Seventy-three plus twenty minus forty-three is fifty. b) One hundred and twenty-
nine divided by three is forth-three. c) Four times twenty-one is eighty-four. d) Edward the
Seventh died in nineteen ten. e) It was exactly eleven thirty-five a.m. on the twenty-first of May.
f) ... three pounds twenty-five pence each. g) ... three oh seven double-two oh one.
h) ... eight stroke two dash double-seven one. i) ... three million, two hundred and fifty-five
thousand, eight hundred and forty. j) I am one eighth French. k) One mile is one point six oh
nine kilometres. l) It is seventeen point three eight per cent gold. m) ... thirty-two degrees
fahrenheit, that is zero degrees centigrade. n) ... two feet six and a half inches by five feet
eight and a quarter inches. o) ... three nil. p) ... two all. q) ... fifteen love ...

Well-Known Spoken Phrases (p.89)

a) Underground station announcer to passengers, or lift attendant. b) Assistant in fast-food
shop to customers. c) Friends or relatives wishing someone happy birthday. d) Court official
asking accused person at beginning of trial whether he pleads guilty or not guilty. e) Customer
asking hairdresser not to cut too much off. f) Customs officer to travellers passing through
customs. g) Owner to dog telling it to keep close behind him. h) Doctor to patient telling him
to get medicine from chemist's. i) Operator connecting caller. j) Customer asking for beer in a
pub. k) Auctioneer when the bidding seems to have stopped. l) Someone announcing a toast to

a newly-married couple. m) Priest at wedding ceremony. n) Witness in court. o) Dentist reassuring patient. p) Someone launching ship. q) Someone at the end of a prayer. r) Someone beginning a fairy-story. s) Photographer asking subject to smile. t) Crew member telling everyone to get on ship. u) Someone shouting that someone has fallen from ship.

Colloquial English and Slang (p.90)

1 Lend me a few pounds. I have no money. Here's a five-pound note. Wonderful. Thanks. **2** Where's my thing that I can't remember the name of? Someone whose name I've forgotten has it. **3** Do you like your new school? It's all right. And the children in your class? They're a pleasant group. And the teacher? Oh, he's a marvellous man. **4** I don't like the new man in the office very much. Yes, he's a bit of a conceited person. He uses his position unfairly. Yes, if I get any more trouble from him, I'm going to tell him what I think. Be serious. You haven't got the courage. You'd be dismissed. **5** High-class suit! My grandparents' 50th wedding anniversary. We're having a bit of a celebration. Come and have a drink first. At my expense. Just for a moment. Mustn't get there drunk. **6** You look a bit depressed.What's wrong? Someone's stolen my umbrella and it's pouring with rain. Oh, bad luck. **7** Saw a film the other night. A man falls in love with a girl, then discovers she's dying. Bit of a sad, emotional film. I suppose it was quite unoriginal and sentimental, but I liked it. Mary Major had a part in it. She must be nearly 70. **8** I think my old dilapidated car's worn out. I'll have to get a new one. Yes, it does look a bit too old to be of any more use. What'll you get? I quite like the new Rover. High-class, grand! It'll cost you a lot of money. **9** Someone's stolen my glasses! Don't be silly. You've got them in your hand. Oh, yes. I'm going mad. **10** I'm afraid the new secretary's completely useless, Joan. The redhead with the fashionable clothes. You're right. She thinks she is someone very special, but in actual fact she's a bit unintelligent and slow to understand. Yes, her work's poor and as you say, she has a high opinion of herself. She's very snobbish, supercilious with the other staff. Do you think we ought to dismiss her? I'm afraid so, but she'll be extremely upset.

Miscellaneous

Geo-political Names (p.94)

1 a) England is only one part of GB. b) GB includes England, Scotland and Wales. UK comprises GB and Northern Ireland. c) British Isles includes GB, all Ireland and all other islands in the area. d) 'Continental Europe' normally refers to mainland Europe, especially central and south. e) The Middle East is roughly between Egypt and Iran. The Far East is China, Korea, Japan etc. f) The subcontinent includes India, Pakistan, Bangladesh etc. g) America means US. North America also includes Canada and, technically, Mexico. h) South America is the land mass south of Panama. Latin America also includes Central America and Mexico. i) Arctic is north polar region. Antarctic south. j) Australasia includes Australia, New Zealand and other islands in the area. k) Southern Africa includes South Africa and neighbouring countries. **2** a) Arabic is normally only the language. b) Scotch normally refers only to products of Scotland. e.g. whisky, beef. c) Oriental = Eastern, Occidental = Western. **3** a) The Netherlands b) Persia c) Burma d) Ceylon e) Eire f) Ulster **4** a) European Economic Community countries (most of Europe) b) Most countries of old British Empire (Canada, India, Australia etc.) c) North Atlantic Treaty Organisation (US, Canada, most of W. Europe, Greece, Turkey) d) Caribbean Islands of Trinidad, Jamaica etc. e) States round the Arabian/Persian Gulf. f) Underdeveloped countries of Africa, Asia and S. America **5** a) US b) Australia c) Japan d) Ireland **6** a) Pakistani/a Pakistani b) Peruvian/a Peruvian c) Thai/a Thai d) Scottish, Scots/a Scotsman, Scotswoman, Scot e) Turkish/a Turk f) Philippine/a Filipino g) Swedish/a Swede h) New Zealand/a New Zealander i) Lebanese/a Lebanese j) Danish/a Dane k) Dutch/a Dutchman, Dutchwoman l) English/an Englishman, Englishwoman m) Iraqi/an Iraqi n) Spanish/a Spaniard o) Finnish/a Finn p) Belgian/a Belgian q) Irish/an Irishman, Irishwoman r) Bangladeshi/Bangladeshi s) Portuguese/a Portuguese t) French/a Frenchman, Frenchwoman **7** a) Paris b) Chicago c) Venice d) Manchester e) Naples f) Aberdeen g) Milan h) Glasgow i) Liverpool j) Vienna k) Moscow l) Rome

Names and Titles (p.95)

1 a) surname b) first name c) nickname d) alias e) pen-name f) hyphenated name g) maiden name h) pet name i) stage name **2** a) Adm. V.E. Nott R.N. (ret) b) W.P.C. Lockwood c) G.L. Cousins M.A. d) Ms Louise Manners e) Rev. Graham Lee f) Sir Robin Sawyer g) Mrs P. Tucker M.P. h) W.G. Smithson Esq. i) H.R.H. The Prince of Wales j) Jones Bros. k) Z. Wilkins R.A. l) John Fox O.B.E. **3** a) Richard b) Edward c) William d) Albert e) Andrew f) Antony g) Thomas h) Robert i) Elizabeth j) Patricia k) Jennifer l) Margaret m) Jim, Jimmy n) Gerry o) Mike p) Chris q) Joe r) Harry s) Les t) Fred, Freddy u) Pam v) Cath, Cathy w) Sue, Susie x) Di

Innovations (p.96)

mountain bikes: strongly-built bicycles for off-road use; wheel-clamping: use of special 'locks' (by police etc) to immobilize illegally-parked vehicles; microwaves: special ovens which cook food quickly using electromagnetic waves; lap-top computers: portable computers small enough to go on person's lap; electronic tagging: attaching device to goods or person enabling whereabouts to be constantly monitored; cosmetic surgery: operations on face, body to improve appearance; bottle banks: collection points for used bottles for re-cycling; cash-dispensers: machines which give money after insertion of cash card and special number; smart bombs: highly accurate, laser-guided bombs; flexi-time: system of allowing employees to choose own working hours; airmiles: system of obtaining free air travel, distance depending on goods/services purchased; jacuzzis: hot whirlpool baths; phonecards: plastic cards bought in advance for use instead of coins in special phone-boxes; modem: system of transmitting data between computers through phone lines; CD rom: small, laser-read disc giving access to sound, information, pictures

Foreign Words and Phrases (p.97)

1 a) cul-de-sac b) hors d'oeuvre c) carte blanche d) grand prix e) Bon voyage f) chic g) tête-à-tête h) blasé i) rendezvous j) nouveaux riches **2** a) gourmet b) coup c) entourage d) encore e) C'est la vie f) au fait g) avant garde h) début i) façade j) détente **3** a) bon fide b) curriculum vitae c) pro rata d) persona non grata e) ego f) status quo g) vice versa h) post mortem i) per capita j) ad nauseam **4** a) macho b) kindergarten c) siesta d) graffiti e) kaput f) Bravo g) incognito h) blitz i) kowtow j) patio

Homophones (p.99)

1 a) too b) I c) guessed d) waist e) mail f) weigh g) where h) wore i) hear j) pear k) weight l) steal m) board n) sees, seas o) principle p) court q) whole r) sail s) meat t) passed u) blew v) read w) stares x) borne **2** a) rode, rowed b) sew, sow c) reign, rein d) suite e) fare f) bowled g) minor h) dyed i) sought j) paws k) mane l) pail m) bury n) hire o) threw p) mourning q) prays r) sealing s) herd t) scent, cent u) cell, v) coarse w) fined x) idol

Abbreviations (p.100)

1 a) a.m. (ante meridiem), p.m. (post meridiem) b) PC (Police Constable), CID (Criminal Investigation Department) c) Oxon. (Oxoniensis: of Oxford University), Cantab. (Cantabrigiensis: of Cambridge University) d) MP (Member of Parliament), PM (Prime Minister) e) BR (British Rail), BA (British Airways) f) RN (Royal Navy), RAF (Royal Air Force) g) GMT (Greenwich Mean Time), BST (British Summer time) h) BBC (British Broadcasting Corporation), ITV (Independent Television) i) AD (Anno Domini: in the year of Our Lord), BC (Before Christ) **2** a) NHS (National Health Service), GP (General Practitioner), WHO (World Health Organisation) b) oz (ounce), lb (pound), st (stone) c) in (inch), ft (foot), yd (yard) d) Con. (Conservative party), Lab. (Labour Party), Lib. Dem (Liberal Democrats) e) St (Street), Rd (Road), Ave (Avenue) f) BA (Bachelor of Arts), MA (Master of Arts), PhD (Doctor of Philosophy) g) mpg (miles per gallon), mph (miles per hour), cc (cubic centimetres) **3** a) HQ (Headquarters) b) DIY (Do It Yourself) c) QC (Queen's Counsel) d) IQ (Intelligence Quotient) e) VC (Victoria Cross) f) TUC (Trades Union Congress) g) HIV (human immunodeficiency virus) h) VIP (Very Important Person) i) MBE (Member of the British Empire) j) SOS (International distress signal) k) UFO (Unidentified Flying Object) l) CND (Campaign for Nuclear Disarmament) **4** a) VAT (Value Added Tax) b) AIDS (Acquired Immune Deficiency Syndrome) c) NASA (National Aeronautics and Space Administration) d) OPEC (Organisation of

Petroleum Exporting Countries) e) NATO (North Atlantic Treaty Organisation) f) UNESCO (United Nations Educational, Scientific and Cultural Organisation)

Similes (p.101)

1 a) hills b) new pin c) dust d) sheet e) feather f) flash g) kitten h) knife **2** a) drunk b) sober c) poor d) cool e) good f) thin g) fit h) deaf

Proverbs (p.102)

1 a) 3 b) 2 c) 5 d) 1 e) 4 **2** a) 2 b) 1 c) 5 d) 4 e) 3

Euphemisms (p.103)

(other versions possible) **1** a) died b) toilet c) old age pensioners d) dead e) go to the toilet f) was very shabby g) killed. a) overweight and rather unattractive b) be sick c) is not the best cook in the world d) rather merry e) could have been more carefully done f) is a little slow on his feet **2** a) dismiss Miss Farr b) spying c) poor people d) is in bad condition e) fail f) dangerous g) has been lazy. a) was not entirely accurate in what he said b) not very fruitful c) has not a very good record of punctuality d) not of the highest quality e) are not as harmonious as they were f) unwise, take industrial action g) we look forward to prompt settlement of your account h) rather displeased

Britain (p.104)

The election system (a) General Election b) call an election c) constituencies d) polling day e) campaigns f) canvassing g) polling stations h) secret ballot i) stand for election j) deposit k) eligible l) turn-out m) Member of Parliament n) House of Commons o) by-election p) constituents q) proportional representation **The House of Commons 1** a) benches b) Speaker c) debates d) Opposition e) backbenchers f) Primer Minister g) front bench h) ministers i) Cabinet j) Foreign Secretary k) Home Secretary l) Budget m) Chancellor of the Exchequer n) Leader of the Opposition o) Shadow Cabinet **2** a) Government b) Opposition c) Speaker d) Prime Minister e) Cabinet f) Leader of the Opposition g) Shadow Cabinet h) backbenchers **Famous Places** a) the Old Bailey (Central Criminal Court) b) 10 Downing Street (official residence of Prime Minister) c) Westminster (district where Houses of Parliament are situated) d) Buckingham Palace (residence of the Queen) e) Scotland Yard (police headquarters) f) the City (financial and banking district) g) the West End (entertainment district of big cinemas and theatres) h) Fleet Street (home of many national daily newspapers) i) Whitehall (street where many government ministries are situated)

The British Isles (p.106)

1) England **2)** Scotland **3)** Wales **4)** Northern Ireland **5)** Republic of Ireland **6)** Edinburgh **7)** Glasgow **8)** Belfast **9)** Dublin **10)** Liverpool **11)** Manchester **12)** Birmingham **13)** Cardiff **14)** London **15)** Atlantic Ocean **16)** North Sea **17)** Irish Sea **18)** Channel

Word games (p.107)

2 a) dog collar, folk song, jumbo jet, flower bed, family tree, mouth organ, shop lifter, lipstick b) fanmail, fire escape, brainwave, beauty queen, coffee table, house arrest, nest egg, jetlag **4** settee, possess, goddess, assassin, essay, cassette, committee, Mississippi, mattress, suddenness, tattoo, keenness **5** (words in brackets give 'ough' sound) bough (n<u>ow</u>), enough (st<u>uff</u>), ought (s<u>ort</u>), cough (<u>off</u>), though (l<u>ow</u>), through (t<u>oo</u>), borough (<u>mother</u>), lough (<u>rock</u>), hiccough (pick <u>up</u>) **6** a) amusing, comical, humorous, hilarious b) youth, teenager, youngster, adolescent c) muse, ponder, consider, contemplate